THE PRIVATE SECTOR IN THE PUBLIC SCHOOL

Can it Improve Education?

EDITED BY MARSHA LEVINE

A conference sponsored by the American Enterprise Institute for Public Policy Research in collaboration with the National Institute of Education

American Enterprise Institute for Public Policy Research
Washington and London

The American Enterprise Institute is grateful to the Aetna Life and Casualty Foundation for funding the publication of these conference proceedings. The conference Barriers to Private Sector–Public School Collaboration was held on June 2, 1983. It was cosponsored by two study centers at the American Enterprise Institute, Education Policy Studies and the Neighborhood Revitalization Project, in collaboration with the National Institute of Education.

Library of Congress Cataloging in Publication Data
Main entry under title:

The Private sector in the public schools.

Includes index.
1. Industry and education—United States—Addresses, essays, lectures. 2. Education and state—United States—Addresses, essays, lectures. 3. Endowments—United States—Addresses, essays, lectures. 4. Educational equalization—United States—Addresses, essays, lectures.
I. Levine, Marsha.
LC1085.P73 1985   370.19'3   85-1222
ISBN 0-8447-2251-0

ISBN 0-8447-2251-0

AEI Symposia 84B

Printed in the United States of America

304462

Contents

Foreword

Over the past decade scholars at the American Enterprise Institute have devoted considerable attention to private sector initiatives in areas of human need, including health care, neighborhood revitalization, housing, and education. The publication of Peter L. Berger and Richard John Neuhaus's seminal work *To Empower People: The Role of Mediating Structures in Public Policy* initiated this endeavor. A series of volumes on the role of mediating structures followed. *Meeting Human Needs: Toward a New Public Philosophy* (Jack A. Meyer, ed., AEI, 1982), for example, included a description of private sector involvement in education and identified the increasing role of business and industry as a provider of education and training and the developing role of the corporate community as a partner in public education.

Since that publication corporate concern about quality education and involvement with public schools has grown enormously. AEI's Education Policy Studies group has maintained a continuing interest in these developments, specifically, in the philosophical and policy implications of such public-private sector interaction.

The project recorded in this volume was itself carried out in the spirit of public-private partnership—a joint effort by AEI and the National Institute of Education. The competing views of business, labor, academics, and practitioners were developed in commissioned papers and presented at a conference attended by educators, policy analysts, and business representatives.

The presenters and discussants do not challenge the basic assumption that public education is a public responsibility. Given that assumption, they address the question of the appropriate role of the private sector in the public schools. They do not suggest that the private sector should or could substitute for or even significantly augment public funding. Rather, they focus on the potential influence the corporate community can have on public policy in education, the impact of a corporate advocacy role in support of public schools, and the value of programmatic involvement with schools on the local level. Participants go well beyond a recounting of examples of corporate involvement in public education (such as adopt-a-school programs or loaned executives) and address fundamental questions of public sector–private sector relationships, roles, and responsibilities. The philosophical and institutional barriers to partnerships are identified as are such public policy issues as equity in resources for public education and the conflicting interests of the private sector. Finally, the discussants identify a research agenda pointing toward the need for a closer examination and understanding of the implications of business-public school collaboration.

The corporate community has a strong and lasting interest in the quality of America's public schools. Education is directly linked to economic growth, just as universal public education is strongly linked to a democratic free society. Enhancing the roles of the public sector and the private sector in supporting a high-quality public education system will be a challenge for years to come.

WILLIAM J. BAROODY JR.
President
American Enterprise Institute

Contributors

MARCIA F. APPEL is director of communications for United Schools Service, a firm that pursues solutions to global education and training issues. Previously, she managed advertising and public relations strategies for twenty-seven countries in the International Operations Group of Control Data Corporation. Ms. Appel lectures on employment and training and is frequently published in newspapers and magazines.

RICHARD ALLEN CALDWELL graduated from the University of Colorado, Boulder, and received graduate degrees in law and social science from the University of Denver. Active as a consultant and corporate director, he has recently completed projects for the National Task Force on Education for Economic Growth, the Education Commission of the States, the Des Moines Register and Tribune Corporation, and the National Institute of Education. He is now director of the Public Affairs Program at the University of Denver and was recently named special assistant to the chancellor for Strategic Planning.

LARRY CUBAN received his undergraduate degree from the University of Pittsburgh and advanced degrees from Western Reserve University and Stanford University. He has held a number of fellowships and grants, including a John Hay Whitney Fellowship at Yale University and an Alfred North Whitehead Fellowship from Harvard and grants from the National Institute of Education and the Spencer Foundation. He is the author of books and articles on education and frequently consults on this topic. He was superintendent of Arlington County Public Schools, Arlington, Virginia, from 1974 to 1981 and is now associate professor of education at Stanford University.

DENIS P. DOYLE is a resident fellow and director of Education Policy Studies at the American Enterprise Institute. He was formerly director of planning and program coordination at the U.S. Department of Education and assistant director for education finance at the National Institute of Education. His paper "Education Policy for the 1980s and Beyond: A National Perspective" was recently published by the Center for National Policy. He has also written widely on education vouchers and tuition tax credits.

BADI G. FOSTER is president of the Aetna Institute for Corporate Education. His academic credentials include a Ph.D. in politics from Princeton University and extensive teaching experience. He has worked in government as an adviser to policy makers, played a key role in the establishment of two new postsecondary institutions as a college administrator, and served as the director of Field Experience Programs at Harvard. He was assistant director of the John F. Kennedy Institute of Politics at Harvard.

MANUEL JUSTIZ is director of the National Institute of Education, U.S. Department of Education, where he manages the federal government's principal educational research and development agency. Mr. Justiz previously was director of Latin American programs in education as well as associate professor in the department of educational administration at the University of New Mexico in Albuquerque. He holds degrees in political science and higher education from Emporia State University and from Southern Illinois University.

MAURICE LEITER is director of program development, United Federation of Teachers, AFT, AFL-CIO. He has been active in public/private collaborative efforts to benefit the schools for many years. He is also engaged at the programmatic, research, and policy levels in youth employment, job training, and school-to-work transition.

MARSHA LEVINE is an education consultant in Education Policy Studies at the American Enterprise Institute. She was a policy fellow at the U.S. Department of Education and is an experienced teacher. Her recent work has focused on corporate involvement in public schools. She holds degrees from Barnard College and Teachers College of Columbia University with a doctorate from the University of Maryland.

DAVID R. RIPPEY is senior administrator, External Programs, Aetna Institute for Corporate Education. His background includes substantial experience in education administration and in business and education consulting. He holds a B.A. degree from Lehigh University, an M.A. from the University of Connecticut and an Ed.D. from Harvard University.

SUSAN SCHILLING is director of academic products for Control Data Corporation. She has been involved with the development and delivery of computer-based education programs for the PLATO system since 1976 and has been instrumental in the growth of the PLATO courseware product line for K–12 institutions.

NEVZER STACEY is a senior researcher at the National Institute of Education. She has designed and managed research and policy studies that address various aspects of education and training in the work place. Her publications and professional interests include research on corporate and union investment in human resources. Under her direction the National Commission on Working Women was created, bringing together representatives from unions, business, and higher education to examine the problems faced by women in nonprofessional occupations.

CICERO WILSON is a resident fellow and director of the Neighborhood Revitalization Project of the American Enterprise Institute. His studies at AEI are focused on public and private sector strategies for revitalizing distressed neighborhoods. Before joining AEI, Mr. Wilson was the director of research and evaluation at A. L. Nellum and Associates, a minority-owned research firm. He has designed and directed youth employment, delinquency treatment, and education programs that have served several thousand Black and Hispanic youth. Mr. Wilson was educated at Columbia and Harvard Universities.

PART ONE
Introduction and Presentations

Approaches to Private Sector Involvement in Public Education

Marsha Levine

Recently, a number of major reports on the condition of America's schools have reached the nation. Among them are the report of the National Commission on Excellence in Education, the report of the Education Commission of the States Task Force on Education and Economic Growth, the Carnegie Commission report on the High School, and the Twentieth Century Fund report. Each report details critical problems in America's public schools; each recommends specific action to deal with the problems; several reports note the interest and concern of business and industry. As is often the case with such reports, they make official recognition of a problem already felt and often already addressed. Such is the case in education and particularly in the area of private sector involvement.

The private sector is already involved with public schools in a variety of ways, of course: private foundations offer financial support; partnerships join individual schools and businesses; local school systems collaborate with industry; and industry provides training, internships, and summer jobs for teachers and students and gives administrative and financial management assistance. The steadily increasing pace at which partnerships are being created locally, coupled with the issues raised by these national reports, has focused our attention on the question of what potential such collaboration really does have for improving the quality of public schools.

To examine one element of this question, the American Enterprise Institute and the National Institute of Education jointly developed an agenda to examine the barriers and incentives to private sector involvement in public schools. NIE and AEI commissioned six authors to prepare papers on relevant aspects of business-education collaboration. The authors include two corporate representatives, from the high-tech and service sectors of industry; a former school superintendent and academic; a state policy analyst and attorney; an official from a teachers' union in a major urban school district; and a public policy analyst with extensive public school experience. The papers provided a

3

springboard for discussion among the business and education leaders, policy analysts, and decision makers who participated in the seminar held at the American Enterprise Institute.

This introduction describes a conceptual framework in which to view such collaboration, briefly summarizes the papers commissioned for this conference, comments on their similarities and differences, and raises the public policy implications of public-private collaboration in education. It concludes with a summary of questions for research suggested by the authors. The remainder of the volume is devoted to presentations made by the authors and to discussion among seminar participants.

Conceptual Framework for Business/Education Collaboration

Some view private sector involvement in public education as an example, among other private sector initiatives, of a renewed spirit of voluntarism in America. Critics of this concept who question the usefulness of such initiative see it as diversionary, drawing attention away from the scope and seriousness of problems in American public education. They claim, correctly, that corporate voluntarism can neither fill the gap created by cutbacks in education budgets nor correct structural problems associated with school deficiencies.

Others view business-school collaboration in the context of public-private partnerships. For them, a reduced federal role in education creates the opportunity for more local and state decision making and, along with that, an increased need for collaboration between the public and the private sectors.

Still others, stressing the relationship between education and economic growth, emphasize the interests business and industry have in a well-educated work force. In this context, education as human resource development is the focus of interest; some tension often exists between the goals of public schooling and these purposes of the private sector.

In reviewing the papers, I do not intend to identify each of the authors with any one particular perspective. In fact, as I studied the papers, I noted that several authors acknowledge and use more than one framework in their discussions.

The paper on the conceptual framework for business-education collaboration, which I prepared, develops these alternative perspectives in more detail. In addition, it suggests to those involved with business-school collaboration that well-developed analytic frameworks already exist to understand, plan, implement, and evaluate these public-private ventures. I suggest three such frameworks: interinstitutional collaboration, public-private partnership, and a systems approach that emphasizes the ways in which school systems relate to external organizations. Each framework offers a method for identifying a particular cross section of barriers and incentives.

The first framework focuses attention on the effects of environment and history, organizational factors and interorganizational processes, and on the roles of individuals and linking structures.

The second framework of public-private partnerships introduces a more specific set of issues related to balancing private sector interests and public sector responsibility and addresses them in the context of public schools. Three changes stand out as significant factors in the development of public-private partnerships in education. First, the definition of education has expanded beyond the traditional schooling in the usual time frames. This altered definition carries with it implications for shared institutional responsibilities and changes in public policy. Second, structural changes in the economy highlight the relationship between education and economic growth, emphasizing industry's interest in education. Third, demographic changes and a low level of public support for public schools create a need for alliances with the private sector, if the schools are to meet their human resource development goals.

In the third framework schools are seen as one system interacting with other systems in society, that is, community and industry. Changes in one system affect functions in the others. Presumably business-education collaborations can profit from examining those patterns of relationships already developed between schools and external organizations.

This paper offers a rather abstract description of these frameworks and suggests how they may be used, and each of the succeeding authors employs some of these guidelines in his or her discussion of collaboration.

Summaries

Maurice Leiter. Maurice Leiter, director of program development for the United Federation of Teachers, takes a pragmatic view of relationships between public and private entities, business, labor, and government. He draws on examples from history and experience in New York City for the development of a "logic of common interest." Today that common concern takes the form of a relationship between economic development and human capital formation and a recognition of the interrelationship between the public and private sectors and their shared reliance on a prosperous economy.

Leiter identifies the now familiar litany of incentives in the private sector, ranging from the benefits to corporations when they support livable, viable communities, to industry's concern for the skills of its work force. The incentives are "human, practical, and urgent." From the public school perspective Leiter identifies the schools' reliance on a positive climate, community confidence, and solid relationships with the private sector. Schools can benefit immeasurably from the climate of support generated from a show of private sector involvement and interest in public education. This is as important as the gains associated with programmatic involvement: expertise, materials, resources, and perspective. In addition, Leiter identifies the intrinsic incentives associated with collaboration: "satisfaction, a sense of purpose and accomplishment, a feeling that people can make a difference, an awareness and respect for partnership and collaboration." In reviewing these incentives, Leiter concludes, with all due respect to the benefits of programmatic involvement, that the private sector can have its greatest impact at the public policy level through support of budgets that "represent a real investment in schooling."

Leiter discusses barriers to business-education collaboration, and related biases, on the levels of implementation and policy. On the policy level, he identifies some issues that arise when corporations find themselves at cross purposes in their desire to improve human capital and to support public schools, objectives that may conflict with their policies related to fiscal restraint. Attitudinal barriers and stereotyping are also raised as obstacles to collaboration. In addressing barriers to implementation, Leiter points to the need of the business and the education sectors for familiarity with each other and for communication. He details organizational differences and emphasizes the importance of dealing with differences in purpose, which he sees as central or core barriers. He advocates an "honest airing" of these differences—necessary if collaboration is to move forward. Leiter provides us with a "stereotype" and a "prototype" for business-education collaboration. The stereotype offers extremes to be avoided. The prototype meets the criteria he defines as characteristic of successful collaboration. Leiter concludes with a set of questions for future research that should be addressed, with the implication that further exploration is worthwhile.

Larry Cuban. Drawing on his experience as a school superintendent in Arlington, Virginia, Larry Cuban begins his paper with a brief historical analysis of corporate involvement in public schools. He identifies a set of unresolved issues that persist today. Changing the focus to California (where he is now a professor at Stanford University), Cuban challenges the assumptions that he believes underlie the California Roundtable recommendations for school improvement: that a lack of appropriate training in high school causes unemployment; that improving high school performance on tests will produce better-trained graduates; that state mandates and better teaching will improve high school academic performance; and that high technology needs demand major changes in the high school curriculum.

Although Cuban questions the validity of these assumptions, he does not conclude that corporate sector involvement has no potential for improving the quality of public schools. Rather, he argues, in support of the fifth assumption of the roundtable, that business support can play an influential role in helping to restore confidence in public schools. Cuban views lack of public confidence as critically disabling to schools, teachers, and administrators. He sees business as an important political ally to education and the development of corporate-school coalitions as promising evidence of the potential influence of business.

While acknowledging the importance of such support, Cuban identifies the conflicting interests encountered by corporations concerned with both school improvements and corporate fiscal interests, or the conflict between short-term labor needs and long-term national interests. Cuban suggests that such conflict can be transformed into a struggle over core issues or they may be sidestepped altogether by concentrating on peripheral programs. He indicates that such a struggle might be beneficial to schools, but not without costs.

Cuban cautions against oversimplifying problems of improving the effectiveness of our schools. He emphasizes that educational quality must be addressed in the elementary schools as well as in the high schools if we are to improve our high school graduates. In addition to the potential for raising public confidence, Cuban sees corporate concern for thinking skills—or problem-solving skills—as an important objective and one shared by the schools.

He concludes on a note of skepticism: Can business involvement improve the quality of education if we predicate our actions on questionable assumptions about what will work?

Badi Foster and David Rippey. Badi Foster and David Rippey take a corporate view of business-education collaboration. They approach the issues from the dual perspectives of corporate education and training and corporate public involvement. As recently transplanted academics in the corporate community, they highlight the contrasts between educators and business people in education philosophy, policy, and practice. They draw heavily on the example and experience of Aetna Life and Casualty and specifically the newly formed Aetna Institute for Corporate Education, where Foster is president.

They describe the process of collaboration from a corporate perspective. They do this first by developing a picture of corporate education and training. Foster and Rippey note that Aetna, like other corporate entities, does not have education as its central mission. Corporations view eduation as a means to an end; schools, in contrast, have education as their central purpose. The two authors discuss a number of internal or organizational factors that affect corporate education and then address environmental factors affecting a corporation's involvement in public schools.

Aetna involvement in education outside the corporation is organized in three ways—through the institute, through a school-business collaborative, and through its Office of Corporate Public Involvement. The authors describe Aetna Institute's External Programs, which are perceived as integral to its human resources development and corporate public involvement strategies and which have both internal and external goals. The authors present a set of conditions that they describe as necessary for corporate involvement in such a program.

7

Their criteria for collaboration establish a corporate perspective on business-education partnerships with an emphasis on process: accommodation, reciprocity, establishment of standards, and communication. They stress the importance of timing, momentum, simplicity of organization, and complexity of problem. They recognize the need for establishing neutral territory, the role played by intermediary organizations, and the nurturing of relationships. In addition, they recognize the internal requirements of an organization that strengthen its ability to collaborate with external organizations.

Richard Caldwell. Richard Caldwell's paper on legal barriers to corporate participation raises a set of issues that are not commonly associated with business-education collaboration. Caldwell, an attorney, is director of public affairs at the University of Denver.

In his view the most significant legal barrier to corporate involvement in public schools will be "the problem of finding mechanisms for the fair and equitable distribution of corporate resources in aid of education." For the past twenty-five years education policy has focused on the equalization of educational opportunity. The elimination of segregation and disparities in school finance have been the objects of "intense litigation." Caldwell contends that corporate involvement may "well be likened to a kind of 'finance,' that is, funding of a new type that could be subject to judicial review by active courts."

Questions of appropriateness abound on both sides. Can schools legally accept such support? How do we deal with the question of inequity from a business viewpoint? Is it appropriate for corporations to give resources away? These questions may be raised concerning the establishment of private foundations in support of public schools as well as in the creation of partnerships. Caldwell suggests a possible tension between a state's concern for the right to equality of education and its concern for establishing education policy that will promote economic development and productivity. Caldwell further indicates that we should consider such legal issues in a broad social framework—one that encompasses the relationship between education and economic growth and that considers the possibility that such growth may require coordinated public-private action.

Marcia Appel and Susan Schilling. According to Marcia Appel and Susan Schilling, who write as employees of Control Data Corporation, "making computer-based education an integral part of the country's educational system requires fundamental changes in the relationships among education, business, and government." Control Data has actively and directly sought ways to accommodate its concern for the quality of public education with its primary objectives—"to make a fair profit and employ people." One way to achieve these goals is through a partnership approach. Control Data Corporation is involved in a number of different partnerships at all levels of education with many different objectives. The Microelectronics and Information Sciences Center at the University of Minnesota is one such example. Control Data donates funds, facilities, and processing expertise. The educational process is enriched, permitting highly technical research, and businesses reap the benefits of new technology. Wellspring, a Minnesota task force whose purpose is to improve education statewide through the use of computer-based education is another example of industry-education partnership.

Although many examples of successful partnerships may be cited, the authors believe that major barriers still exist. Among such barriers they include resistance of teachers to computer-based instruction because they fear loss of jobs and the resistance of school districts because they fear "de-humanization" of education and excessive costs.

The authors believe that computer-based education can fundamentally change the process of teaching and learning in public schools. Sophisticated development and implementation of such a basic change require extensive private sector-public school collaboration.

Research Agenda

Each of the authors addresses needed research. Together, they present an ambitious agenda for both the private and the public sector.

Foster and Rippey advocate the establishment of a well-developed historical perspective to serve as an incentive to action, as well as to avoid duplication of effort. Also, they address the particular issues related to research on public-private collaboration. Research should be useful to both sectors and usable by both. This stipulation may necessitate new research models to accommodate the ways that each sector uses research and conducts it. The authors raise the possibility of collaborative research. As topics for theoretical research they cite conceptual or policy issues; and for action research their agenda includes the identification of working models for planning and management, implementation, and evaluation.

Caldwell suggests that we need to examine the social framework that may shape the law concerning equitable distribution of resources to the public schools from the business sector.

Leiter's research agenda includes policy questions: How can contradictions of purpose be dealt with? What is the federal role in facilitating corporate involvement in public schools? Are there results possible only through collaboration? Is programmatic institutionalization possible? Are collaborative programs cost effective? What changes in the perceptions of corporate leadership can be identified with private sector involvement in education? What are the effects of internship programs on teachers' expertise, knowledge, and commitment to teaching? Leiter also suggests some basic data gathering on the value of investment, the distribution of resources and money, the tax implications, and the effects of corporate giving to education on other areas of corporate social responsibility.

Cuban's skepticism over assumptions business makes about how it can improve the quality of schools implies a research agenda. The questions are familiar but nonetheless critical. What is the relationship between school achievement and unemployment? How can we maintain a balance among the agendas of parents, professionals, taxpayers, and business in developing school policy? What curriculum changes in high schools are required by high technology? What effective models exist that can help teachers develop analytical skills in their students? Also, Cuban sees a potential for the private sector to raise confidence in and public support for the schools. This potential would be stimulated through the identification and description of successful coalitions that have lobbied successfully in support of the public schools.

Conclusion

The papers are instructive for their similarities as well as for their diversities. Although they do not include the views of all relevant constituencies (for example, the parent-citizen groups or federal policy makers), they articulate a number of viewpoints of business and education. We hope that these ideas will serve as a springboard for discussion among others with a broader range of interests.

The authors raise similar concerns about conflicting interest and cross purposes. They identify organizational and inter-organizational barriers; they see a range of possible effects of private sector involvement in public education. They suggest a number of public policy issues raised by corporate involvement in public schools. The areas of corporate involvement are so diverse that they call into play policy options ranging from teacher certification to school finance. There are equity issues that may arise from corporate contributions, financial and in-kind, to schools and school districts. The state's interests in ensuring equally financed public education must be balanced against its interest in promoting quality education for economic development. Balancing stake-holder interests and influence on public education is a challenge to policy makers at all levels.

While each of the authors recognizes important differences between industry and schools, they tend to think about those differences in ways that themselves reveal differences. The corporate perspective tends to acknowledge the differences and to emphasize processes for coping with them. The academic view tends to identify the differences as barriers. Somewhere in between, labor takes perhaps the most pragmatic view of collaboration.

Whether readers agree with this analysis or with the authors' views, we hope that they will want to examine their own ideas on collaboration and share them in constructive interchange.

Introductions

Denis Doyle, Manuel Justiz, and Marsha Levine

MR. DOYLE: Today's seminar, Barriers to Private Sector/Public School Collaboration, is part of a longstanding tradition at AEI of informed and spirited discussion and debate. In meetings of this kind we want to provide a forum for policy debate, to provoke discussion, and to stimulate the competition of ideas. Although AEI takes no position on issues, we believe that the important topics of the day warrant your attention and interest. We think collaboration between the private sector and the public schools is one of those topics.

Today's seminar is also special, perhaps unique, in one important way: its organization and funding provide a counterpart to the subject matter before us. Five of the papers were commissioned by the National Institute of Education and one by AEI. As well as being a collaborative effort between AEI and NIE, this seminar also represents an intraorganizational collaborative effort between AEI's Education Policy Studies division and its Neighborhood Revitalization Project, directed by Cicero Wilson.

We are riding the crest of a wave of public concern about education, which makes today's meeting even more important than it might otherwise be. Recent reports of the past month—the Report of the National Commission on Excellence in Education, the Twentieth-Century Fund Task Force Report, the Education Commission of the States Report, chaired by Governor Hunt and cochaired by Governor duPont and IBM's Chief Executive Frank Cary, and the College Board's Report Project EQuality—all derive from a widely shared belief in both the public and the private sector and a concern that American education is in deep trouble and that we must now, as a nation, turn our attention to improving it.

We are happy to have with us Mr. Owen B. Butler, chairman of the board of Procter & Gamble and chairman of the Subcommittee on Business and Education of the Committee for Economic Development. This subcommittee is undertaking a major study of this area, the results of which will be available soon.

Dr. Manuel Justiz, director of the National Institute of Education, is also with us today. The life blood of policy analysis and informed decision making

11

by policy makers is high-quality research: the federal government plays no more important role in education than in supporting the National Institute of Education. It is a pleasure to cosponsor this event with Dr. Justiz, and I now turn the program over to him.

DR. JUSTIZ: All too often public education and the private sector have been on separate and, at times, narrow-gauge tracks. With the recent, intense coverage given to the findings of the National Commission on Excellence in Education, we sense a great awareness of the need for all segments of our society to "merge tracks," to marshal our resources to overcome what may seem insurmountable obstacles.

As attested by AEI's sponsorship of today's seminar, the private sector and education are vigorously attempting to respond to the challenges and recommendations set forth by the commission report. Certainly one of the major points of the report is that technology can be infused in all aspects of learning as opposed to just one area, a concept the National Institute of Education wholeheartedly endorses.

Since coming to the institute, I have initiated a long-range program in technological research. We have already developed the framework of this ambitious project, along with a number of target dates for the implementation of various projects.

Probably one of the most exciting elements of our educational technology initiative is its private sector component. With the secretary of education we are putting together a national study group to consist of approximately twenty people, about three-fourths of whom will come from high-tech industry. Educational technology provides a good opportunity for educators to work hand in hand with the business community in developing and refining the research agenda and in forging a cooperative partnership.

During the coming months at the National Institute of Education, we will begin building that partnership with the private sector. We will work in concert with it to address the challenges that the institute and our country face in education, particularly as these challenges relate to educational technology.

In still another tangible way the private sector and education tracks are merging. The papers commissioned by AEI and NIE explore the nature of many of the rules, regulations, court decisions, and laws that affect the degree to which the private sector can aid public education. The papers, which represent various perspectives, are meant to be exploratory and, I trust, will be the catalyst for a lively and fruitful discussion.

If public education is to thrive, mutual trust must evolve between public and private sectors, and public-private partnerships must be encouraged. Our cooperative efforts need to go beyond the activities of the institute.

We need to support the initiative President Reagan has taken in encouraging private industry to adopt schools, and we must encourage educators in turn to work closely with the private sector in addressing the challenges we have in education today. This is where NIE research and today's conference come in: we wanted to look at the incentives and the impediments to collaboration between education, labor, and industry.

We want your ideas on administrative procedures, legislative initiatives, school policies, state standards, and the like, which you feel either help or hinder such partnerships. We want your recommendations on ways to eliminate road blocks as well as on ways to encourage interested parties in developing cooperative partnerships.

Finally, we want to assure you that our research capabilities are available to assist you in any way possible in order to meet this important goal.

DR. LEVINE: The question underlying today's discussion is really what potential public-private partnerships have for improving public education. In addressing that question, we have focused on collaboration between the private sector and the public schools as one form of corporate involvement, looking at barriers to the formation and successful implementation of such partnerships.

I see collaboration as just one strategy for private sector involvement in education, and it has some special strengths. Such collaboration bears directly on two important problems in education: the isolation of schools and the weak communication links between sectors. Collaboration is, however, a complex form of involvement.

Our objectives today are to use the exploratory papers as a basis for discussion. We are interested in understanding people's concerns about public-private partnerships. We are interested in recognizing and identifying real and perceived barriers to partnerships. We are interested in defining existing and potential incentives for partnerships. Finally we are interested in finding areas for further research on partnerships.

The papers presented here will give a cross sectional view of barriers to public-private partnerships. Each author has identified implementation barriers, organizational barriers, and policy issues relevant to collaboration between the private sector and public schools. In addition, each author has a particular view on these barriers. Two of our authors give corporate views, one speaks from the perspective of an academic and chief school administrator, one explores a labor-education viewpoint, and one author presents legal aspects.

My own paper provides the most general discussion of the issues and offers what may be a useful structure for identifying barriers to collaboration and for understanding the other presentations as well.

A Conceptual Framework

Marsha Levine

Events of the early 1980s have emphasized the strategic importance of education in America's economic development and have placed education high on the nation's agenda. At least three dramatic changes in the American economy point toward greater dependence of business and industry on the quality of the public schools.

First, global competition will increasingly require American industry to work smarter, faster, and more efficiently. To do this, employees need to be able to adapt to technological change in the workplace.

Second, a shift in our economic base from smokestack industry to information-based, high-technology industry has created an increasing demand for better-educated workers with knowledge and skills in mathematics, science, and technology.

And third, to maintain our leadership position in these new industrial areas, we depend on highly skilled individuals to keep us on the "cutting edge" of new technologies through research and development.

Increasing attention is being directed toward understanding the relationship between education and economic growth and documenting the costs of educational failure. Business and industry, recognizing their dependence on the output of the public schools, are seeking ways to affect quality in public education. Business-education collaboration represents one such attempt.

It may be no coincidence that at the same time that business and industry, in self-interest, are asking how best to improve American public education, there are signs of positive change in the schools themselves: higher standards are being reintroduced; requirements for promotion and graduation are being reconsidered; and student performance levels in some areas are going up. Such signs of encouragement are evidence to the outside community that efforts for improvement are worthwhile. They offer a seriousness of purpose to the questions central to this paper: What is the potential for private sector-public school collaboration? Is it a viable way of improving the quality and relevance of public education? What are the barriers to its success?

The object of this paper is to increase our understanding of the potential of such business-education partnerships or collaboratives by suggesting three frameworks through which they may be considered. The first way of looking at private sector-public school partnerships is through the conceptual framework of interinstitutional collaboration. The most general framework of the three, it provides us with a way of assessing these joint ventures. The second framework is that of public-private partnerships. More narrowly focused, this framework presents a set of questions and raises a group of issues related to balancing private sector interest and public sector responsibility in the arena of public education. The third framework to be applied is that of a systems perspective: the interaction of schools, workplace, and community. In this last view we will concentrate on school-business partnerships as one example of how schools relate to external organizations generally.

These three frameworks provide an increasing degree of specificity. There are obvious overlaps in issues and approaches, but each framework adds a perspective of its own. They each offer the opportunity for useful insights about business-education partnerships and are suggested as fruitful areas for further examination. Examples of how the frameworks can be applied to existing collaborations should illustrate their utility and encourage further, more in-depth analysis. Before applying these three frameworks, however, we need to say a few words about collaboration as a strategy—its peculiar strengths and its potential for achieving the ultimate goal of improving public education.

Forms of Collaboration

Corporations involved in collaborations or partnerships with public school systems provide financial support, links to community resources, curriculum development, teacher development, advisory and planning assistance, and budget and management expertise.

These activities have several purposes: to facilitate school-to-work transitions; to develop career awareness; to encourage business, economics, or free enterprise education; and to strengthen basic education, as well as curriculum in specific areas of science, mathematics, and technology.

Involvement takes many forms: "adopt-a-school" programs, curriculum development projects, teacher in-service programs, or participation in magnet school development. Some have short-term objectives; others reflect long-term commitments. Some collaboratives are initiated by the school systems, others by corporations or universities. A considerable number of collaboratives are the result of court mandates related to desegregation decisions. Collaboration in Boston, Cleveland, Los Angeles, Denver, Dallas, Providence, and Buffalo is the result of such court orders.

At the outset we should recognize that collaboration between industry and public schools is just one of several strategies that the private sector may

15

employ in an effort to affect the quality of public schools. Other strategies include direct funding through corporate donations and political support through lobbying for public funds and supporting legislation. In addition, corporate policies that encourage parent and citizen volunteer activities may lend support for public schools without requiring direct institutional involvement.

Collaboration here is defined as relationships between organizations, involving sustained interaction between members of each organization and including the identification of shared and agreed upon goals. Collaborations or partnerships have taken many forms. Further application of the conceptual frameworks identified in this paper should be helpful in understanding why some forms are viable where others may not be and why some forms of collaboration arise where and when they do. Moreover, they should assist us in understanding how the characteristics of any collaborative may determine its limitations.

Partnerships or collaboratives are different from other strategies for private sector involvement in their requirement for direct interaction between the corporation or business and the schools. Herein, perhaps, lie their greatest strength and also the source of their greatest problems.

In terms of potential, collaborations can produce two critical changes that go to the heart of school-to-work transition problems. The first change is to counter the isolation of schools—an isolation felt by the individual classroom teacher and typifying the policy-making process at all levels. This isolation is detrimental both to schools and to the complex systems that influence economic growth. Although the systems may labor inefficiently but more or less adequately during stable periods, times of crisis emphasize weak links. The enormous education demands of an economy in transition from a manufacturing base to an information-services base cast in high relief the need for education-private sector collaboration. Public education needs much closer ties with the economic community if it is to achieve successfully its goal of human resource development. Similarly, business, industry, labor, and commerce cannot address the requirements for growth and increased productivity without considering the resources of education and the responsibility of the education community for policy, planning, and implementation. Collaboration, therefore, achieves the dual purpose of moving education out of isolation and involving it as a strategic component in economic planning.

A second and related change that collaboration may facilitate is the improvement of communication between schools and the private sector. Improved communication serves at least two purposes. Identification of the skills and knowledge required by employers is one of the most important components in bridging the gap between education's outcomes and industry's needs. The communication of this information is critical. There are significant problems associated with what gets communicated and how. Collaboration or

16

partnerships may represent the opportunity to establish effective, ongoing links that would ensure this necessary communication.

Another aspect of improved communication through such collaboration is the direct effect it can have on students. Up front, visible corporate sector involvement in public schools can link students to the reality of the workplace and provide the critical connection between what happens in schools and what will be required on the job. The importance of these changes cannot be overstated. Reduced isolation and the strategic involvement of education in economic development, together with strong communications links between the schools and the private sector, can lead to significant changes in both education and industry.

Going Public: A Labor-Education Perspective

Maurice Leiter

We are all here to take advantage of a tremendous opportunity. Whatever hair splitting, fine points may be raised, we have a chance to create a universe of stake holders in public education. We have never had such a chance before. We bring together resources and intentions more serious, more genuine than we have ever had in modern history. We must not lose this opportunity. Let us hope that we are already a group of stake holders who share certain common goals.

We should approach this issue in a very serious way, that is, in the intellectual arena as opposed to the merely political arena. Although political arguments for collaboration abound, I think the rationale for this approach derives from fact, from knowledge, from research, and from relations in our society. That is my approach. I do not believe that the increasing involvement of business with public schools is merely a bandwagon phenomenon. It may, of course, have been accelerated to some extent by certain political developments. Long after those political developments have been forgotten, I believe that the value of our coming together will still be with us.

The experiences of the fiscal crisis of New York City are illustrative. Despite its extreme negative effect on education, human services, and the ability of that city to survive, that crisis brought together public and private sector interests, banks, pension funds, corporations, unions, and others to work collaboratively.

Although one might argue that the greatest sacrifices were made by the labor movement—and we might even be able to substantiate that claim—it also seems fair to say that all of us developed a strong pragmatic sense about what it takes for a city or a society to survive and what the intricate links are between the economic health of an environment and its social and educational health.

It was a bad experience but a good lesson for us. We also came to understand that cynicism about the motivations of others is not productive, but rather we must find the logic of common interests in what we undertake. And I see genuine common interest in this type of undertaking. It embodies the view that our actual or potential economic prosperity is part of a continuous whole. The public sector draws its support from a viable economy. The flow of tax revenues from that economy, to which it contributes in turn, yields an educated populace capable of contributing to continued growth and development. The private sector, in supporting substantial investment in public education and training, reaps the benefit and the productivity of its skilled employees and the purchasing power of, we hope, a prosperous population. One sector nurtures the other in a continuous cycle.

In a long section of my paper, I conclude that the incentives for such collaboration are in the public domain. They are known to almost everyone. Obviously, a corporation doing business in a city has a strong incentive to strengthen the public school system, create stability in the community, create a flow of employees, encourage middle management and other personnel to take up residence in the city, and, in general, create a harmonious environment for its employees.

Furthermore, a better-educated and skilled population will be a more creative and productive work force. Resources invested in human services and human development can support constructive efforts instead of simply compensating for social deficits—crime, unemployment, neglected health, and the like. We exist in a very practical context. Moreover, if we look ahead, we find that a literate, skilled population capable of flexibility and versatility is what we will require in the decades to come.

A citizenry less dependent and less prone to obsolescence will be less likely to be among the legions of dislocated workers that our society now has. Change demands that people be able to adapt, and only education can create that capacity.

Moreover, we will soon enter a period when demand for workers with both sophisticated and simple skills will outdistance the supply of new entrants to the work force. We cannot afford to neglect or underserve those segments of the population that have been least served, least educated, and most dispensable. We can no longer tolerate the numbers of older workers who languish because retraining opportunities are lacking or ignore the unmet needs of adults whose illiteracy makes them unemployable. We also need to serve the hosts of disadvantaged young people, primarily of minority origins, but also the rural and urban white poor, whose potential is more staggering than any technology; the millions of handicapped whose strengths and promise far exceed their handicapping conditions; and a large cohort of women of school age and otherwise who need to be assisted into the mainstream of society.

All these people make up both the problem and the solution. They will be your workers, your citizens, and your producers in time to come, if we provide that opportunity. At the same time, they will be your consumers; they will be your prosperous population about which I spoke.

We are talking about a kind of marriage, then, of human resource development, of economic development, and of education; these have always been the basis of growth in our society. The difference is that now we are beginning to see that we can work more effectively if we do it together.

We must not forget, of course, that significant barriers may hinder such an undertaking. One of the basic barriers is bias—the baggage that each sector brings with it in confronting the other. Typical examples of such bias would be "business is interested in the public schools for selfish purposes," "school people don't understand the real world," "business involvement is antihumanist," and "public education is a disaster." Those are just four typical expressions of bias. To my mind, however, the recognition of the barriers is a step forward in overcoming them.

We all know that we can find selfish businesses and disastrous schools. That is not hard to do. We also know, however, that when we look closely at the reality of what a corporation is undertaking or what a school is grappling with, we begin to see the quality and the texture of the real world of each one's endeavor. At that point we begin to see that no simple stereotypes apply to the situation.

As we work together, we begin to respect each other's needs, problems, and strengths. Overcoming this kind of bias is no different from overcoming any other kind of bias. It is true, though, that some things are a bit troubling. One of the great burdens that the private sector has in this context, for example, is avoiding actions seemingly at cross purposes. In my paper I cite Atari, which, on the one hand, offered grants of computer equipment to schools and, on the other hand, closed plants in Sunnyvale and San José moving 1,700 workers off the rolls.

San José is broke right now; a very upward, forward-looking school system has been economically crippled, in essence. Atari's concerns and motives in moving to the Far East are obvious: to manufacture cheaply and to be competitive. I recognize also that the micro actions contradict their macro actions. This example illustrates the dissonance in the private sector's point of view.

In contrast, a very selfish motive can yield a very positive outcome. Our organization has worked creatively and productively with the leadership in Time Inc. in New York City and the Education Committee of the New York City Partnership, of which Mr. Timpane chairs the Working Group. Time Inc. has a very wholesome, selfish interest in literacy, and I see nothing wrong with forwarding that interest by constructive activities to create a literate population. I do not consider it undesirable to serve one's own interest and serve the public will at the same time. In fact, that is probably the best way to bring people together.

There are some intricate problems in addressing a public-private sector relationship—problems of differing social organizations and differing senses of what constitutes productivity, measurement of outcomes, and the like.

Let me turn to what I consider the nub of the matter and describe some characteristics of collaboration. If organizations or people are to come together for a common purpose (and finding the common purpose is one of the reasons for coming together), the parties should not arrive with rigid predispositions. The situation must proceed from a basis of equality. Everyone is an equal within the process. All goals and processes are jointly developed, and actions evolve from consensus, not power. Self-interest belongs out in the open, and everything is negotiable. No party to a collaboration should be asked to commit suicide, so to speak, to further someone else's particular goals. People have needs; institutions have needs; a corporation, a school, a union all have certain needs. These needs must be respected.

The art is to build out of a mutuality of interests to serve each other. Each partner will not have the same thing to give. If you are rich and I am brilliant, then I have to give with my brain, and you have to give with your wallet. If neither of us is rich or brilliant, then we should broaden the base of collaboration.

Parties to good collaborative relationships experience great new respect for a sector, an area, or a universe that they never understood before. They begin to understand that, fundamentally, it is not institutions that are coming together, but human beings that are coming together. Human beings are motivated to succeed and to be relevant to what is undertaken.

In conclusion I want to comment on what I see as the most powerful role that the private sector can play. In my own experience in concrete, substantive relationships with the private sector, I have witnessed some beautiful examples of collaborations that have benefited schools, employers, communities, and others. In the last analysis, however, we are dealing with a national issue, and we are dealing with public policy issues. The most powerful influence we can have is to support the kinds of initiatives that make a public education system strong enough to carry our society forward in a time of great competition and almost paranoia about our supremacy, both as a nation of entrepreneurs and as a nation of human beings.

Corporate Involvement in Public Schools: A Practitioner-Academic's Point of View

Larry Cuban

The current enthusiasm for business-education collaboration is neither unexpected nor novel. It is not unexpected because school districts are deeply involved in the business community on a daily basis and share a number of common interests concerning efficient use of public funds and concerning civic obligations to produce an informed citizenry. Finally, it is not unexpected because schools have historically served as handy targets for reformers.

It is not novel either. It is not novel because there is a rich history of previous coalitions of industrialists and educators since the 1890s that have not succeeded in vocationalizing the high schools' curricula and have not succeeded in vocationalizing citizen expectations of what schools should do.

Also, the current enthusiasm is familiar because periods marked by a conservatism—the 1890s, the 1950s, and the 1980s—share a similar concentration on gifted students, on more academics, and on outdoing foreign competition. The current enthusiasm, therefore, may be predictable to informed observers.

Examination of the assumptions underlying the present desire for this collaboration reveals a blend of claims and facts in an attractive set of political trade-offs. Some of these trade-offs may enhance public schooling, some of them are peripheral, and some of them may prove detrimental. In my paper I identify and examine at length five assumptions drawn from a report of the California Business Roundtable, a very impressive group that I feel is representative of the present thinking on the collaboration of business with schools.

The first assumption is that lack of appropriate training in the high schools causes unemployment. The complexity of economic forces in this culture, the complex equation that produces unemployment, forcibly argues against the simplicity of that assumption, however. Structural unemployment in heavy industry, demographics, corporate mismanagement, and foreign competition—all contribute to the complexity of the unemployment problem. Pointing an accusing finger at the high schools as the cause of unemployment seems quite simple minded. High schools, of course, play a part in that equation, but we are facing a multifaceted phenomenon and cannot afford to single out one particular group as the precipitating force.

The second assumption is that improving high school performance on tests will produce better-trained graduates. The limits of standardized tests and their restricted use as a surrogate for predicting future worker productivity argue strongly against the wisdom of equating test performance with skills in the marketplace. The passion for numbers and quantification of complex issues runs throughout society, and test scores, which are important in a limited way, seem capable of arousing expectations far beyond what they can deliver.

The third assumption is that state-mandated standards will improve high school academic performance. Stiffer graduation requirements, tougher teacher certification and evaluation standards, and a longer school year influence the general conditions for academic improvement, but they remain quite distant from direct influence on classroom teaching and student performance. In my judgment, to suggest that such mandates at the state level will improve classroom instruction, student test scores, and the marketability of graduates is promising far more than can ever be delivered. Such expectations will only set up another cycle of disappointment in the schools.

The fourth assumption is that high-technology needs require major alterations in the high school. In my opinion, rather than rushing to renovate the high school curriculum to keep pace with computer technology, we should be cautious in making sweeping changes.

The fifth assumption is that business support will help restore confidence in public schools. Here I believe that business-education coalitions can promise much improvement in the current low state of public trust in the schools. The pivotal role that public schools in this culture play as a social glue holding together loosely connected institutions can be reasserted and dramatized by corporate/school partnerships. This is a more modest assumption than the other four. In my view, however, it is more promising than the other assumptions behind the thinking of the California Roundtable.

I count myself as a mild but skeptical enthusiast of the current passion for corporate involvement. I believe that public policy makers need far more caution in striking a balance between the conflicting purposes of public schooling, the insistent demands of different constituencies, and professional judgments about what is best for students.

Equity Issues in Corporate Support for Schools

Richard Allen Caldwell

In this paper I raise some questions about how much oversight of public/private partnerships, in terms of course review, we can expect as these partnerships develop. The critical issue is how we are to make the legal system—the system of courts interpreting the Constitution and making public policy—responsive to our concerns with respect to the use of corporate resources in the public schools.

This is no simple matter. In my opinion it boils down to the question of equal protection. I phrase the question thus: what do equal protection and due process—both as general terms and as terms with specific constitutional denotations—mean in the context of public/private partnerships? That is, how do we avoid entangling judicial intervention in the formation of public/private partnerships? This will not be an easy question to resolve.

The question is not necessarily easy even to think about, because it involves fundamental American values and fundamental legal concepts.

The first value, of course, is *equity*, the second is *fairness,* and the third is *equality*. What do those words mean in terms of participation of corporations in the public schools?

The key here, from a constitutional standpoint, is that as corporations participate in the schools, they are involving themselves, along with the public schools, in a form of state action. The state action requirement is necessary for judicial review on an equal-protection basis.

The central question can be phrased in the following way: how do we find the constitutional mechanisms for the fair and equitable distribution of corporate resources in aid of education? In this paper I have argued that as corporations participate in the schools, we must avoid a sense of unjust enrichment. That may be, for example, unjust enrichment of one group of students who occupy a particular socioeconomic class at the expense of another. Or it may be the unjust enrichment, as I have also argued, of a group of students who happen to live in one school district as opposed to another school district.

It is productive when we think about these questions of equity to make some analogies to the school finance cases that have been with us since the early 1970s. To what degree do we see education as a fundamental right? If education is in fact a fundamental right—and some state courts have said that it is—then certain consequences follow in terms of equality of corporate efforts.

If, on the contrary, education is something less than a fundamental right, then I think we have a great deal more flexibility regarding potentially reviewable corporate actions. Philosophically at least, we need to take a moderate view of just how far we can extend or should extend the due process and equal protection clauses of the Fourteenth Amendment as we consider corporate participation in the schools. We need to balance the right of individuals to an excellent education against the interest of the community, of the state, and, in a more constitutional sense, of the promotion of better education.

In a technical or legal sense, it is obviously in the state's interest to promote better education. It is also a right of students to something approximating an equal education and certainly to an education that partakes of the concepts of equity and fairness.

In summary, I want to emphasize two things. First, because these issues will be increasingly important, we must pay attention to the due process and equal protection problems posed by public-private partnerships. Second, at this point it seems unnecessary to jump to the extreme of predicting that a court will interpret every action of a corporation in aid of education strictly according to the Fourteenth Amendment. We cannot look at public-private partnerships in a legal vacuum. If the history of judicial intervention indicates anything over the past several decades, it is that courts will be very interested in issues like this, particularly when the life chances of real people are affected by actions in both the public and the private sectors.

One Corporation's Commitment to Quality Education

Susan Schilling

The relevance of corporate involvement with the schools is obviously very great to all of us. The relevance of this involvement to Control Data is very clear, because we are in the business not only of developing products with the educational community, but also of selling them to that community.

Most of my remarks pertain to our cooperative efforts for the educational environment. Then I will describe where we are at Control Data, where we have been, and where we think we are going in terms of the issues as I see them.

The idea of a joint venture cooperative partnership is not a new one to the corporation. Most of our cooperative work has occurred with other private organizations rather than with public sector institutions. Over the years our chairman has followed a philosophy of cooperation wherever possible with hardware manufacturers. Most recently, this philosophy was evidenced in the formation of a group called Microelectronics Computing Consortium, established to help deal with the competitive threat from the Japanese. This effort pools research and development dollars from the high-tech industries.

In applying that same philosophy to the public/private enterprise, we have obviously run into many of the issues and barriers that Maurice Leiter alluded to in his paper. It has been an interesting enterprise, and we have been at it for almost twenty years now.

As those of you familiar with Control Data know, we have directed most of our effort to a computer-based educational division with the PLATO products. Our first real cooperative effort was with the University of Illinois in the 1960s with funding from the National Science Foundation. We attempted to develop schools with teachers trained to be effective in a computer-based environment. We have gone a long way since then.

To digress briefly, I want to share with you the basic philosophy of corporate responsibility that distinguishes Control Data.

Mr. Norris, Chairman of Control Data, is probably the most pragmatic idealist any of us will meet. He firmly believes that research is important. He also believes, however, that the only way to know the effect of a new technology in a changing environment is to try it.

According to him, the philosophy of our corporate social responsibility is to try to work with the technology in the particular environment, an effort that leads into long-range strategic planning and eventually into long-range profits for the corporation.

We have redirected our efforts somewhat since the first ten years of corporate social responsibility. Formerly, Control Data gave money in grant form to institutions, either colleges or elementary and secondary schools for specific pilot projects.

Recently, our cooperative ventures in development and delivery of materials have evolved to the point where both the public and the private institution have a vested interest in the success of those efforts. We are, of course, very happy to see this change.

The basic strategy of our approach to grants to the public community is to use the strengths of both communities without duplicating either of them. In other words, our goal is to educate a population that will serve both the public and the private sectors. What we need to do to reach that goal is to build on the strengths of the individual institutions.

The public education sector has the creative talent, has the intellectual ability, and knows how to teach the subject matter. Control Data has the ability to distribute the product of that effort nationally and even internationally. We can also help equalize access to information and technology to avoid problems raised in some of the other papers.

In the long run, we have seen a change, a positive one I believe, in terms of our educational grants, our educational philosophy, and our public/private partnerships. In the past, we concentrated on nontraditional areas. We worked in the prisons, we worked on the Indian reservations, we conducted joint efforts, wherever possible, with the Minnesota State Department of Education. On one particular occasion a grant from the Bureau of Education for the Handicapped supported development of courseware. At that point we could not find a school willing to work with us, even though we were giving away the equipment. The biases and a natural reluctance of some educators to accept technology explain this hesitation. The fear of losing a job, the fear of change, and the lack of hardware in the schools also hindered cooperation. Positive changes in all those areas have taken place.

Before I close I want to look more closely at scenarios of two specific marketplaces—one elementary/secondary and one postsecondary—where some of these partnerships are now active. Recognizing a problem in retaining the best and the brightest of their teachers, representatives of a local school district in Minnesota came to us. They feared losing good teachers to industry, basically because of inequities in pay. They proposed a joint development

27

effort. The school district would provide the educational expertise, the educational methodology, the intellectual content, and the testing ground for the materials. We would provide our synthesis of market research on the "hot" topics nationwide, guidelines for courseware development, and tools to help them write programs without having to learn programming. We would then distribute the product for them. Royalties would come back to the district for distribution to the teachers who helped develop the product, thereby giving them additional income.

The partnership at the postsecondary level is newer and probably bigger. We are offering our lower-division engineering curriculum as part of a cooperative engineering program. This venture has attracted some publicity. Our purpose is to bring the power of the PLATO learning experience to about 110 postsecondary institutions in the lower-division engineering courses.

Seven major universities have cooperated with us in the development of these materials, and 110 universities are now cooperating with us in the delivery of the materials. Again, this is a significant change from several years ago.

In conclusion, if I have concentrated on our recent success rather than on our previous lack of success, I did so because I hope we have learned from some of our failures. We certainly see public-private partnerships as a wave of the future, and we hope that the policy discussions resulting from this forum will lead to some very practical applications.

Corporate Responsibility in the Context of Rapid Change

Badi G. Foster

I am an academic. I have spent fourteen years building institutions of higher education and working in public schools. I think I have a sense of the public side of education, and in the last eighteen months I have been on the corporate side of it.

Working together with David Rippey on this paper has provided a very useful opportunity to step back and reflect on some of the questions we are busily supplying answers to whenever the issues of corporation education, training, jobs, and young people surface.

I would like to provide briefly some specifics to help us understand the debates that I suspect will ensue when we discuss papers by Mr. Cuban, Mr. Leiter, Mr. Caldwell, and others.

First of all, Aetna, the context within which we operate, is a large financial services company of some 50,000 employees. A third of them are situated in Connecticut, and the rest are scattered around the United States. This company is undergoing a series of fundamental transformations, and I use "transformations" deliberately. Let me list them briefly.

First, Aetna is transforming itself from an insurance company into a financial services company. That is like changing from the railroad business to the transportation business.

Second, we know that technology has both intended and unintended consequences. We are IBM's largest customer. We have twenty-five full-time IBM people assigned to us, and nobody except the Defense Department purchases more magnetic tape. A company that uses the number of personal computers we do changes its means of production and invites other consequences.

Third, although the company has traditionally viewed itself as a domestic northeast-based corporation, it is now making a leap into the twenty-first century, becoming a financial services company in a global economy. The consequences of that kind of movement for the people in the company are absolutely enormous.

29

As we view those transformations—and corporations in general—in the context of Western civilization, we have to acknowledge the genius, at least in American society, of creating the limited liability corporation at the turn of the century and to do so in such a way that the corporation takes on a life of its own. Society accepted limited liability corporations on the grounds that such a mechanism is the best arrangement for generating an economic surplus that can be distributed in an efficient and equitable fashion and thereby leaven the whole society. If we accept this assumption and the fact that corporations today—while performing primarily economic functions, increasingly perform social, political, and ethical functions—then we must ask ourselves, What is the proper role of a corporation in this society in the latter part of the twentieth century?

These considerations bring us to the notion of public-private involvement. This involvement implies more than social responsibility. It has to do with the very way in which companies design their products and conduct their business, in addition to whatever philanthropy that they might be involved in. If we expand the concept of corporate-public involvement beyond social responsibility to include the educational dimension of responsibility, then we can understand how the company came to see that corporate-public involvement would necessitate establishing coherent relationships with "those publics outside the company."

In addition, in the nature of our business it is neither the technology we acquire nor the assets we manage that determine our prosperity. Indeed, it is our people. We are, therefore, greatly concerned to give the same amount of attention to the development of our human capital that we give to other forms of capital. These conclusions are the basis for the Institute for Corporate Education, which will be the central educational force within the company and the vehicle for development of our human capital—first and foremost for the 50,000 people who worked with us and second for those public entities, particularly those with whom we do business. I would like to make five major points.

• First, as far as Aetna is concerned, education and training are not our central mission. We are in the business of providing financial services for profit. Therefore, education and training are viewed, unfortunately too often, as an expense, as overhead, but, I hope, increasingly as an investment.

Because education is not the central mission, however, we decided to try to link our Institute of Corporate Education with other educational institutions—the public school systems, particularly in the City of Hartford, but also, in the beginning, with institutions of higher education in Connecticut. We make this connection in the hope that eventually the educational programs necessary for our employees can be found in institutions that have education as their central mission.

- Second, within Aetna, program quality and quality control of education take precedence over public policy concerns in corporate decisions on public-private partnerships.

- Third, successful collaboration involves intra-institutional as well as interinstitutional arrangements. To the extent that a corporation has not developed coherent arrangements within itself, the possibility of entering into useful and successful collaborations with other institutions diminishes. The Institute for Corporate Education, then, will allow us to marshal, with some degree of coherence, the resources and people within the company so that we can find a way to collaborate with others.

- Fourth, we believe that some "neutral turf" or buffer zone is essential to any successful collaboration between business and education. This is particularly true when that collaboration requires multisector participation, not only the schools, not only the labor unions and the businesses and the parents, but community-based organizations.

- Fifth, in any form of business-school collaborative the parties need to accommodate competing definitions of "the problem." (Mr. Cuban has alluded to this as has Mr. Leiter.) Too often, people think that there is one acceptable, legitimate definition of the problem: for example, youth and unemployment or the transition from high school to work. We have found that obviously there are competing definitions.

If within that neutral turf one accepts and encourages the articulation of those competing definitions, then in the long run one is more likely to agree to pragmatic and effective activities with some chance of success. These small successes will have a cumulative effect.

Let me close with an analogy. At the end of the nineteenth century and the beginning of the twentieth century, the degree of nationalism in the world was extraordinary. The nation-states were so afraid that collaboration with other countries would undermine their autonomy that they resisted any attempts to create international bodies. Yet people recognized that it would be convenient to send letters across international boundaries and that if they sent letters to each other, they needed stamps and that somebody must design a system so that one country does not pay all the freight. Literally, the solution to a specific problem led to the creation of the International Postal Union. As key nations participated in that joint effort and enjoyed its advantages, they began to see potential in other areas, such as disease control, where collaboration could also produce obvious benefits. Thus, the idea of the World Health Organization was born.

With incrementalism, at the local level in particular, we may create effective and efficient school business collaboratives where we have failed in the past.

PART TWO
Discussion

Response to Presentations

Marsha Levine, moderator

RICHARD A. CALDWELL, University of Denver: My question concerns corporate goals. Since 1887 when the Interstate Commerce Commission was founded, our regulatory system has aimed at restricting the negative aspects of corporations. In other words, we have been concerned with a kind of negative duty concept. Now, however, we are hoping to move beyond the concept of just social responsibility; we are not going to harm society by polluting the water or selling impure hamburgers, or the like. We are moving toward an affirmative concept, in which a marvelously flexible notion of corporation is about to take another major step forward.

We are beginning to recognize the potential that corporations have for positive contributions to society. This concept is very different from the negative view, which holds that society must be protected by stringent laws from the potential abuses of corporations. We want to explore the affirmative role of corporations in a very complex society. I think that that concept recasts the argument quite a lot. Would you comment?

MAURICE LEITER, United Federation of Teachers: I think we have to get past social responsibility, corporate social responsibility, and the vice-presidents with that title. I think it is a gross embarrassment to sit behind that kind of title because, it separates a person from the main business of the firm. Within corporations the commitment to other than direct profit-making activities has to be part and parcel of the mission. Mr. Foster was trying to get at that in discussing social responsibilities like philanthropy in the context of his corporation's activities.

I also appreciate the thoughtful reserve of Mr. Cuban's paper. To me the important thing about the California Business Roundtable is that it is not on the outside but on the inside of a major issue. The members of the roundtable are willing to go to bat to raise money and to raise standards in schools. They are willing to make a commitment and get right into the middle of it, and they are reasonable to expect something sensible in return. And our position has been—and this is an organizational position, not only mine—to communicate and, in

35

the process of communicating, to find that common ground. We expect to give as well as to get and through that process to accomplish our goal.

CICERO WILSON, American Enterprise Institute: Before the conversation becomes further involved in the structure of the relationships and the partnerships, I would like to bring up several other issues. We have talked a lot about these public-private partnerships . . . and they are very important. We should not forget, however, the role of parents in the process of forming public-private partnerships. How can two institutions (school and business) so distant from the parents in the education process unite and at the same time avoid increasing the gap between the parents and the schools?

We must examine the purpose of the partnership and the strategy, not just the barriers. I am reminded of what my father used to tell me about traffic lights: "Don't watch the traffic light," he would say, "because the traffic light never hit anybody. Watch the traffic." One finding from our neighborhood research (we call it the Light Brigade finding) is that it isn't leadership that is missing—it's strategy. In talking about how these partnerships are structured, we have to be careful to talk about their purpose and about how the structure facilitates the purpose.

I would also like to take issue with Mr. Cuban on the five points from the California Roundtable. He agrees with the last one, which states that corporations can help build a respected image of public education. Harshly put, it is almost like the blind leading the blind. Surveys taken from the mid-1960s through 1980 rank the medical community at 50 percent, the top in terms of public confidence. The education community ranks 39 percent. People have strong confidence in the education community. The military ranks along with the education community at 39 percent. Corporations rank 25 percent, and Congress ranks 19 percent. Labor ranks last with 15 percent—labor leaders have the confidence of only 15 percent of the general public.

Given the greater confidence of the public in schools than in corporations, can corportions support the image of public education? It is very important to recognize that both education and corporations have an image problem. There are many good schools; there are many good corporations doing a lot of good work. Just to mention one effort, in New York City cooperative education in the 1981–1982 school year provided $25 million in wages to 15,000 students.

Polls show that the general public is not aware of these sorts of ventures. If they hear about them, the knowledge often drops out of their consciousness. It will take a lot of work to raise public awareness. Collaboration will give the corporations an opportunity to improve their image, and it will give the public schools an opportunity to improve their image. The bottom line, however, is that many people do not see that leadership in either of those institutions corresponds to their needs. I wonder how specifically corporations will improve the image of the public schools. Part of it is effectiveness, just getting a better product from the schools.

BADI FOSTER, Aetna Institute for Corporate Education: No amount of packaging and repackaging can take the place of actual concrete results, the fruit of one's labor, if you will. Your point ties in with something that Mr. Cuban raised in his paper: the accusation often made that corporations want to change the high school curriculum so that they will have a better work force.

Mr. Cuban's point is that we really ought to be talking about a higher level of critical thinking skills rather than about more vocational skills. The financial service industry is an information industry. Our traditional entry-level cohort comprises high school graduates that we train. We are, of course, concerned about the issue of remediation, and in fact devote enormous resources to remedial assistance.

What we really need are those critical thinking skills because change within the company is so rapid that we must have individuals with both the will and the capacity to absorb and generate persistent change. Although that sounds theoretical and abstract, it really comes down to pragmatic questions. One of the ways we get to know each other and to understand the problems driving us is through collaboratives.

In reference to Mr. Wilson's question, as we understand our environment, then perhaps we can be more creative in designing ways for parents to be effective or in finding a new role for a community-based organization.

I will close with this metaphor: in the insurance industry, we flew on automatic pilot for about twenty years. All of a sudden we hit clear-air turbulence and are now bouncing around the sky trying to get our hands back on the controls. Perhaps our industry is peculiar, but I doubt it.

Educators who understand the changing industrial environment must use their special wisdom to develop a high school curriculum more responsive to the real needs of industry.

ROBERT CRAIG, American Society for Training and Development: Mr. Leiter, I would like to comment on something you mentioned—Atari's move to the Far East. It is often implied that Atari maliciously decided to move. I think we should look at the motives, however. The decision must have been reached only after a great deal of soul-searching. What was the choice—to move to the Far East and survive, or stay in the United States, lose a lot of money, and lose the jobs anyway?

What Dr. Foster describes is something that we should keep in mind when we talk about education/work relations. The issues are not easy to pin down, and I think we have to work hard to keep this process continuing. It is getting worse. It is not a simple matter of remediation but a whole set of complicated issues. What is needed in Hartford may not be what is needed in Albuquerque. And it probably isn't.

We have a very complicated situation here, but I think the name of the game is change. I would like to stress that.

BRAD BUTLER, Procter & Gamble: Two comments, if I may. First, I would like to underscore what Mr. Foster said. The Committee for Economic Development Design Committee, as it addressed this subject, was unanimous on the point made by Mr. Foster, that what industry needs from education is teaching the ability to learn, not teaching a skill, for exactly the reason cited: that technology is changing the nature of jobs so rapidly that young people coming out of the schools now will need to be able to learn a new job every several years.

Schools are a mirror as well as a shaper of society, and all of the papers that I have read on education lately have ignored the first role. They recognize the role of schools in shaping society, but fail to recognize that they are first a mirror of society and that many of the broad problems in education may not lie in the educational system but in the society, and as Cicero Wilson has said, in the parents. The schools have to do what the parents want them to do. Many of the problems perceived as national are in fact societal rather than educational—not all, but many.

Then, Mr. Craig touched on the fact that the school problem is not a national problem: it is a local problem. The schools in the Cincinnati area, for example, are totally different. There is no relationship between the problems of Hughes High School and the problems of Indian Hill High School, and certainly there are not the same problems in the high schools of Harlem and the high schools of Louisville, Kentucky, or St. Louis, Missouri. These are individual. This is one of the reasons the opportunity for business cooperation is important. Businessmen are pragmatic, more concerned with a specific local school's situation than they are with the national problem. I suspect that the solution to many of our problems will come from that approach.

I would underscore what Mr. Cuban said, that we do need a good deal more research conclusions and a good many fewer assumptions and hypotheses about what is wrong with the system. We need to know more about what we are doing, and we need a clearer definition of what we mean when we talk about the school problem.

My final comment concerns corporate social responsibility. Mr. Leiter, you will be happy to know that not only do we not have a vice-president for corporate responsibility, we do not even have a board committee for corporate responsibility. We do not know how to dissociate our corporate responsibilities from what we are because we believe that it is the corporate responsibility and enlightened self-interest to serve the shareholders, and that it is improper for a corporation to undertake anything contrary to or not in the self-interest of our shareholders. But that definition of self-interest has to be enlightened; it has to embody a very long-term, broad view. With that definition, it is easy to act from a positive sense of corporate responsibility rather than from a negative sense.

ROY FORBES, Education Commission of the States: I want to add a comment to those just made. The work of the Task Force on Education and Economic Growth has been a round-robin type of thing, with business people, educators, governors, and so forth all educating each other. Through our experience we have found that the business community wants educators to impart two specific things. First is the ability to continue learning skills, the ability to adapt, to participate successfully in on-the-job training or in the training institutes run by companies and businesses to teach people new skills.

Second is to develop certain attitudes in students and young people, so that when they leave the educational setting and enter the work force they show up for work on time, get along with coworkers, and get along with the people they are working for. They need a set of attitudes as well as a willingness to learn skills.

The first time we met with a group of business people I expected a great deal of conversation about the basic skills, and we spent about five minutes talking about them. Business people, however, were not very interested in discussing the basics; they wanted to get rather quickly to the learning skills after the first hour and a half of discussing attitudes.

In my frequent talks with education groups around the country about what is going on with the business-education collaboration, educators express two fears that I think are unfounded. One is that business people are interested in taking over the education enterprise, that they want education to respond to just their needs. In our work with the business community, they seem to be saying to us, "We want to help; it is in our best interest to help you. But you must tell us how we can help. What is it you want us to work with you on?"

The other fear educators express is that some government bureaucrats will move in with their quick fixes or that someone will pass a piece of legislation purporting to solve the problem totally. When people make very simple assumptions, they often propose very simplistic quick fixes. It occurred to me, Mr. Cuban, as I listened to your comment, that some might have feared that response from the group of governors and legislators that we have been working with. That fear has been disappearing for me.

We need to bring government, education, and community leaders together to establish that neutral ground, that buffer zone that Mr. Foster talked about within his corporation. As these leaders work together, they can respond to the challenge, understanding that we face a long-term problem and not a problem solvable by passing a quick bill to give loan forgiveness to a group of science teachers in Kentucky, for example.

LAUREN WEISBERG, Connecticut Business and Industry Education Foundation: It sounds as though the business community wants these higher-level skills. I do not think anyone would argue with that statement. The kinds of contributions that businesses are giving to schools are very specific. They seem to be targeted to learning computer skills or specific remediation skills.

It seems to me that often the larger decisions companies make about the bottom line may have a negative effect on the general funding of education. In Connecticut I have seen tax policies, supported by corporations, that take money away from the schools. This forgone tax money would probably have gone to fund the general level of education. How does that situation play itself out? How does one make these broader-level decisions to support general learning as opposed to funding specifically targeted projects that are easier to get approval for?

MR. LEITER: That is really where the issue is: thousands of projects throughout the country engage corporations with schools. Some are remarkable, and most of them are local-level projects. In New York they are called "join-a-school," and in Los Angeles they are called "adopt-a-school." They involve technical systems loans, resources, or people speaking on various occupations. They offer work experience, vocational experience, coop-ed—it is a remarkable array. Some of these have been around long before we started talking about them. They are terrific, and they are not going to solve the problem. This is where some of us might part company, because the problem is in public policy and involves knowing where self-interest really lies.

Earlier, I used the Atari example, not because I disliked its commercials or because I think it did something unusually egregious or specious; I understand its motives. I was trying to identify the relationship between micropolicy and macropolicy, not because I have a ready-made conclusion, but because it is the knottiest of all the problems that we face.

Understanding the relationship between micropolicy and macropolicy will expand our concept of what constitutes enlightened self-interest, and it will be translatable into the prosperity of businesses. The macrocosm will fall into line with the microcosm. Right now they are not really together except in a very few instances, but where they are together, we have our very best outcomes.

I am not against local efforts; I am not against them at all. They have been very helpful.

If we had another seminar, I could mention many examples of really productive local activities. But they will not change anything; they will only enhance local situations. What will change something is the public policy posture.

MICHAEL TIMPANE, former director of the National Institute of Education and president of Teachers College, Columbia University: I have been talking about several new laws of social behavior that we are inventing here. One is historical antideterminism, meaning that nobody is in control of the environment anymore. That is a serious, pertinent commentary on why very important forces are drawing people together in all kinds of aggregations.

I am comforted to hear from Mr. Foster that Aetna hit clear air turbulence, since the schools have thought for many years that that was a normal state of the atmosphere. I believe that our society at large is just now experiencing a readjustment to the fact that nobody is in charge. Nobody feels in control of things as in the past. I believe the situation calls for new arrangements—or at least they seem new to us—now sprouting up in every area of our mutual endeavor.

The second law of social behavior I call the fallacy of highly educated opinion: "In general I don't like the public schools, but I like the one I've got." In every public opinion poll I have seen, people may be critical of schools in general, but they like *this* school, they like *our* school, or they like *my* school.

MR. WILSON: Not in the neighborhoods that I've been studying.

MR. TIMPANE: No, but it's even relatively true there—relative to schools in general. People say, "My school is somewhat better than I think schools are altogether." What these comments indicate is the absolute importance of the substantive and solid local connections. Mr. Leiter knows that I agree with his point that policy discussions are essential and that new policy compacts are going to be a very important part of any satisfactory future.

These compacts, however, will rest on quicksand, at least from my observation of the state of preparedness and experience of many corporate officials entering this arena. The compacts will rest on quicksand if they are not thoroughly grounded in local, very practical, very easy incremental steps and successful experiences to start with. I think a sequencing is needed to carry out these concerns to the policy level and successfully sustain our efforts there.

JACQUELINE DANZBURGER, Institute for Educational Leadership: I have worked in the area of education and youth employment at the local level in Hartford, Connecticut, and am familiar with Aetna. One of my concerns is the fusion of effort. We have many projects that exist outside the mainstream of the educational institution; it is easier to do that. Somehow we hope that this effort will feed back in and have an effect on the mainstream of students, of staff, and of the organization of the system. It is a rare community that could cite evidence that this has happened, even when it is supposedly built into the design as with magnet schools.

We are making demands that assume that we can control the outcome. I think state legislatures will begin to move in this direction, but we must look at the capability of the schools, where the capability lies with the human re-sources. Just as corporations are concerned about investment in their human resources, so must schools be.

For this decade the staff supposed to deliver the product demanded is not there, in part because of RIFs, an aging population of teachers, and indeed the lack of resources for staff development. Although I have not researched the subject, I would guess that most corporations—while they have given a great many gifts to higher education, especially to train people for management, science, technology, and the like—have rarely given comparable money to the schools of education or even recommended specific ways for strengthening them.

This may not be in the realm of public policy. In the corporate board room, however, there could be policy discussions around the relationship between schools and corporations, corporate resources and ways they might affect both teacher education, higher education, and school systems in the staff development area. I do not think we can wait for "trickle up" in terms of what happens in individual schools. We must take it on as a large issue.

DR. FOSTER: I want to respond to Ms. Danzburger's concern. When we created the Institute for Corporate Education, a $50 million educational facility equipped to match anything now available in terms of educational design and technology, I became one of the most popular and feared people in Connecti-cut. The question was, "My God, are they going to offer a degree?" With a market of at least 20,000 people within the two- or three-state area, I could operate very well, and my good friends at the University of Hartford and other places were very much concerned. We created a joint advisory committee with some eighteen presidents and heads of government bodies of higher education in Connecticut to meet with us once a quarter to discuss ways in which we might collaborate. We did that as a way of trying to communicate our inten-tion. One of the unintended consequences of this collaboration is that the people from the community colleges, the state technical colleges, and the state universities who were furious with each other and would never be polite and civil had to sit for about three hours once a quarter to talk about what they have in common.

That certainly was not our primary intention. It appears, however, that the regular contact is forcing educational leaders to start to develop a consensus. This might begin to answer the question that Ms. Weisberg raises about the appropriate public policy for the corporate sector to support, based on the consensus derived from education leadership.

A second underrated issue on the table is the question of equity that Mr. Caldwell raised. That is a very serious issue, and, quite frankly, I had not thought it through until I read his paper. We have made a clear commitment to cities and urban areas and to directing our resources to those least well served.

We think we have the best intentions and that we are right in line with other kinds of reforms in school finance. Two years from now, though, we may find ourselves party to a legal suit that we had not anticipated. That possibility causes some unease, and we may need to collaborate on research of that issue.

My third point concerns school reform. In the late 1960s and early 1970s, school finance reform was viewed as a way of correcting some problems in our society. In one instance the Ford Foundation pumped money into Florida to create a marvel school reform finance law and a bureaucracy to go along with it. All of a sudden, in the state of Florida legislators began to play a new and interesting role in determining what the formula for such reform would be.

Can you imagine business people, urged to get involved in public policy, playing that same role in education? The involvement of business in making education policy may be an unintended consequence but one that we ought to talk about before we act with the same enthusiasm and good intentions that we had concerning school finance reform.

MICHAEL USDAN, President, Institute for Educational Leadership: I certainly applaud Mr. Leiter's statesmanship in trying to move into the intellectual realms and not the political realms.

My fear, however, is that unless the schools recognize the demographic realities, they will indeed become very marginal institutions in our society because so much of the action has already shifted and continues to shift away from our traditional institutions. If one believes the projections of Pat Choate, and other economists, for example, 90 percent of the 1990 work force is already employed and 75 percent of the 2000 work force is already employed. We lack the luxury of two or four or six years of study, debate, and conceptualization of the problems.

The moving target that Mr. Craig described is moving so quickly that nobody can keep track of it. As I move around the country, I become more and more confused by the changes that the traditional educational institutions at all levels are encouraged to make, both for substantive and for economic reasons as well as for political and demographic reasons. The tempo of this change suggests that it is not business as usual for anybody in the society.

This message may be a little more urgent for educators because most of us grew up in those halcyon days of the 1950s and 1960s. We have a leadership who came to maturity when everything was expanding. Nobody knows how to preside over decline very well.

What concerns me so much, if one looks at the demographics, is that the schools cannot make very many assumptions about public support. They need to go out and reach constituencies. There is a sheer pragmatic need to do that in terms of survival, with the demographic realities of population, a younger population that is an increasing minority, and an aging population that is an increasing majority. I feel an urgency about alerting traditional schools to this reality, not only relative to their own survival and viability, but also relative to the cohesion of the whole social fabric. Yesterday was too late. I cannot overemphasize that the demographic trends force us to face reality.

MARCIA APPEL, Director of Communications, United Schools Service: We at Microelectronics Computing Consortium now have many local projects of our own going on. We get together with other companies and universities. Our decision to open new locations has generally been influenced by the availability of good schools and a pool of engineers and good graduate schools nearby.

In response to the point that schools should examine demographic trends and the need for workers to be retrained every ten years, if not every two, I would cite the study to be undertaken by a school in St. Paul this year. This school is becoming what we have described as a community outreach resource. It will serve as a focal point for the transfer of technology and new learning skills into a larger community.

RITA KAPLAN, Honeywell, Inc.: At Honeywell I conceptualize, design, and implement some of our educational programs in the community. I am interested in the very practical matters posed by partnerships and collaborations.

We need to be aware of the leadership requisites to collaborate in an effective partnership. Leadership must come from school districts as well as from corporations. It also takes commitment and staying power, because collaboration in a partnership does not develop overnight. It is a very long developmental process.

Yesterday the Minneapolis and St. Paul Chamber of Commerce granted Honeywell an award for a programmatic magnet that we set up in the Minneapolis public schools in a partnership program. In a newspaper article on the award, a reporter quoted a teacher who said, "We really don't know what to do with Honeywell."

Now, one year into the project, it is going well and is considered one of the best designs. The trouble with partnerships, however, is that you really have to keep working at them. I do not think that teachers who have been isolated from business really know how to use our resources, and we do not know what resources we have that they can use. We obviously need more communication. As we learn what each other's needs are, we will see complementary elements, the areas of common domain, and the contributions the other can make. That is another issue that takes a long time.

I also have an observation on the training issue. In our educational system, human resource development, or in-service training, is very narrow. People learn how to teach a course or how to write the curriculum for a course. Teachers are not provided the kind of developmental opportunities that we have in corporations. This is the training that builds your soul and allows you to survive when you are working against all odds. We are trying to implement programs to do that for teachers.

44

My final comment concerns culture. That has been a key word in corporations in the past five years: understanding corporate culture. If corporations want to be involved in the education community, they should understand the educational culture and work with educators to help them understand what the culture is, what they want it to be, and how we can use some of our resources on their behalf.

BOB WOODSON, National Center for Neighborhood Enterprise: Although I am a latecomer to this field, I question some of the underlying assumptions I hear expressed. In our talk about collaboration among megastructures of the society—institutions, education, and corporations—we tend to see education policy as a captive of these structures and to assume that developmental opportunities improve training, in other words, improve transactions among these megastructures.

What is the source of innovation that will bring about improved education for kids? And it seems to me that we ignore an important resource that Cicero Wilson alluded to earlier in his remarks: much innovation occurs within low-income communities and informal institutions. A proliferation of private school options are being pursued by people who are organizing themselves, and some are doing so at great personal sacrifice.

These people are not crazy, although in a sense they seem to be. In one family we interviewed, one fellow works in a laundromat, and in another the father drives a truck. They spend $6,000 of their disposable income to put their children through private schools in their own community. If those parents are making that kind of sacrifice for alternative private schools, what is going on there? Won't these community-developed, innovative school alternatives affect the attitude of young people toward learning as well as toward the skills which are imported? How do we then factor these possibilities into discussion and policy?

I am reminded, as someone said once, that the Harvards of this country can never alone solve the problems of the Harlems of this country. The question, then, when we talk about collaboration, is how we factor in the innovation occurring within the smaller units of society. How do we begin to glean from these communities and from those institutions information that can perhaps direct alternative policies of the future?

MR. FOSTER: I don't know if I can give a complete response to Mr. Woodson's question. I happen to think that the Institute for Corporate Education that has emerged at Aetna is, first of all, an innovation. As demographics shift and more adult learners need education and training more closely connected to the work site, this type of institute will begin to spin off other kinds of innovative structures.

Our building was built with an Urban Development Action Grant, even though Aetna Life and Casualty does not need federal dollars to build a

45

building. I would guess that behind that decision lay a desire to connect our work to the megastructures such as the federal government. To construct such a building, then, incurs not only legal responsibilities to be of service but also moral responsibilities.

Yesterday I met with Lynn Gray from the New York Urban Coalition and Brian Rollins, who have formed a joint venture called Coalition Mountaintop. In this organization the Urban Coalition is now beginning to market skills that it has developed related to race and agenda issues. The profits from this consulting venture are pumped back into housing, health, and other programs for which the Urban Coalition could not find funding. If that idea could be applied to Hartford and a way found to provide resources to an innovative community organization, some alternatives might materialize.

Just as those small firms produce most of the new jobs, not the Aetnas, it is small neighborhood organizations that may be key to providing services in counseling and in education that could support an institution even as large as the Aetna Institute.

I would close with this: there has to be commitment, as Mrs. Kaplan suggested. There is a difference between commitment and contribution, though the two tend to get confused. The difference is captured in the plate of bacon and eggs: the chicken made the contribution, and the pig made the commitment.

Organizations and people have to decide whether, in terms of education of adults and young people, they are prepared to make a commitment or a contribution. There is room for both, but the failure to make that distinction leads to raised expectations and discouragement.

SOL HURWITZ, Committee for Economic Development: As I listened to this conversation, I thought back to my experience in the early 1970s as a member of a local school board. It occurred to me, Mr. Leiter, that if you are talking about the micro level, that was as micro as you could get. In the context of this discussion on public and private collaboration of business and the schools, however, not once as a board of education did we seek out the representatives of the corporate community in our suburb to ask them for their advice on the future direction of the school system. I should also add, not once did the representatives of the corporate community seek out the board of education except in its role as a supplier that wanted to sell us various products and services.

The problem is not only one of bias—and I agree that bias is certainly a factor—but one of inertia. There was no particular reason why we neglected the business community, just as I am sure there was no particular reason in those days why the corporate community did not seek out the board of education. One of the barriers to collaboration, it seems to me, is sheer inertia. Now, how do you overcome that inertia? I suggest that what every system needs is an intermediary. I see a real need for an individual, an institution, or a mediating

46

force to bring those two sides together to overcome that inertia.

The public sector and the private sector do not always speak the same language. Although common forces may bring them together out of self-interest, out of a common need in a community, we need an interpreter or an interlocutor to translate the needs of one in terms of the needs of the other.

We have some impressive representatives of such mediating organizations sitting around this table. We have not heard from Dave Bergholz, but I think the Allegheny Conference is one of the preeminent mediating organizations in the area of school/business collaboration. Every community needs someone or some organization that will help bring the two sides together for truly effective collaboration.

PETE WEAVER, District of Columbia Public Schools: In response to the issue of barriers to productive collaboration, I point to a lack of communication. Teachers have been teachers most of their lives, and business people have been business people most of their lives. They live in two different worlds and work in two different styles. Although business does need to understand schools better, schools need to understand business better. If I invite you to lunch, I pick up the tab. If schools are asking for business to help, it is incumbent on schools to learn the language and the style of business.

How do we accomplish this? I think it comes through teacher exchanges, internships, and other interchanges that put teachers and principals in productive positions in industry and put industry people in the classroom. Communication is the beginning, and without it you cannot have an effective partnership.

MR. WILSON: My first comment concerns the learning-to-learn skills. A survey done by the Center for Public Responsibility showed big perceptual differences between what the schools thought they were providing and what business thought that it needed from the schools. I think that is one issue that needs further research.

I would like to ask this group, Is there a public-private partnership in education designed specifically to give youths learning-to-learn skills? Does anyone know of one? I have seen compendiums of business-school partnerships that deal with a multiplicity of things, usually targeting a specific career such as engineering, word processing, or whatever.

From my perspective in neighborhood economic development, I see many corporations looking for opportunities to make contributions, but the strategy is not clear. This is one of the gaps. What do you do in the classroom to transmit learning-to-learn skills? The only program I know about is 70,001, which teaches communications skills to young people.

MR. LEITER: In my paper, the positive example of collaboration that I use and describe at great length is the Mastery Learning collaborative in New York

47

City, with the Economic Development Council, which is now the New York City Partnership. The Mastery Learning Project strategy is, in effect, a learning-to-learn approach for the young, as well as for the teacher, in terms of the analysis and organization of instruction. This is one example of a significant, well-established, and successful public-private collaboration that deals with both learning-to-learn skills and the basic skills at the same time.

MR. WILSON: As I see it, a lot of school systems are still looking for what to say when they are asked, "What can our corporation do for you?" They do not have a ready strategy on hand.

MR. LEITER: That is part of the collaboration. I do not think we should point out something that should become the bandwagon for corporations.

MR. WILSON: I see a conflict, then, between saying that what is needed is learning-to-learn skills and saying that you do not focus on strategies.

MR. LEITER: Learning-to-learn skills will be the outcome of the successful, productive educational system. If we do all of the things suggested today, including the staff development activities that both Ms. Kaplan and Ms. Danzburger mentioned, we will provide resources for teachers and support from those collaborators to build the skills and to improve the critical thinking of the students.

MR. WILSON: In program design, though, I see a big gap between the techniques mentioned for broadening teachers' in-service training and specific outcome. I do not think a direct line has been constructed between what is intended or is needed and what the actual implementation strategy is.

MS. KAPLAN: I have a partial answer. I think public schools have to do some homework. Let me cite an example in Minneapolis. Four corporations took the leadership along with about nine other corporations to put together around $100,000 for the Minneapolis public schools to do some long-range planning. As a result of this long-range plan, the schools began to understand what the issues were and what corporations could provide for them.

The plan set up five committees, cochaired by corporations, to work around those issues. In my view, you address these problems through strategic planning and by giving the schools the facility to assess their own needs rather than by having the corporations assess what they think they should do for the schools.

JOAN RATTERAY, National Center for Neighborhood Enterprise: How do you overcome the problem of accountability, or the expectation of accountability, between two megastructures that ordinarily have different ways of looking at accountability.

For instance, when a corporation gives something to a school, how long does it take to find some results? In what way do you judge how well the contribution will be used or how successful the partnership is?

MR. TIMPANE: It seems to me that if the contribution is accompanied by a presence and by continuing relationships, the issue will not arise. The corporate officials will be in the school from time to time and will understand either: (1) what the effect is; or (2) why it is not realistic to expect that the effect can be isolated. If you make a contribution without involvement, you will raise that issue. To me, though, the involvement is just as important as the contribution itself.

MARSHA LEVINE, American Enterprise Institute: At this point I will hand the moderator's job over to Nevzer Stacey from NIE. She will lead the discussion into research issues, which is one of our objectives for the seminar.

Research Issues

Nevzer Stacey, moderator

NEVZER STACEY, National Institute of Education: The National Institute of Education is the research section of the Department of Education. We have been working in education and training in the private sector to understand what is going on with the so-called "third-sector providers," organizations that provide education but whose main mission is not education.

As we continue this discussion, let us focus on areas in which NIE, as a federal research agency, could conduct research. We are, of course, a very small speck in this universe, and our studies will not provide answers by tomorrow. We can, however, offer some incentive for others to explore these issues. We can form collaboratives to generate discussion, encouraging other people to join the debate and advance knowledge in the field.

As I looked at the papers, I saw that each one raised questions that could be turned into topics for research. One, for example, mentioned the importance of considering this collaboration from a historical point of view. The need to restore confidence in public schools might be put in a historical perspective. The question is, Is there evidence that when institutions collaborate the result will really restore the confidence of parties involved?

Are there predetermined factors? In other words, if your goals are quite clear and if you can achieve those goals within the agreed time, then does that successful collaboration raise the esteem of both parties?

Although many questions might afford us intellectual exercise, we can also address many practical matters. What happens, for example, when schools are in dire need of financial assistance and the corporations lend a hand? I am thinking of a school that received financial assistance for training a specified number of high school seniors for jobs as bank tellers after graduation. I wonder if those people will still be bank tellers in that community two years from now? Did the parties consider the possibilities? How short term are the bank's needs? We have raised the expectation of the people by training them when there may not be any jobs. Is this a good way to get together? What are we doing in those circumstances?

EVE KATZ, American Council of Life Insurance: I would like to respond to the

50

last question. As a trade association, my organization plays an intermediary role in bringing our member companies closer to local secondary schools. I put together a group of representatives from companies with experience in collaborations with local high schools. It was interesting and surprising to discover that far less evaluation occurred than I would have anticipated.

Perhaps this reflected a certain bewilderment over how to go about such a task. It may also reflect a limitation of the commitment that the company sees itself capable of making. If a company could evaluate this activity more effectively, maybe it would make a greater commitment because of greater confidence in what it was doing.

This avenue might then be more fruitful in encouraging businesses, which traditionally and understandably like to measure results. Likewise schools, as they enter into this mode of collaborative activity, will themselves lose heart if they cannot see and understand the results of the collaboration. From both sides, then, it seems to me that more careful evaluations would be worthwhile.

In addition, we might give some attention to the source of the initiative and to what degree that affects the nature of the collaboration and its success.

Speaking as a representative of an intermediary body, I would find it of some interest to see whether initiatives take on certain coloration or have certain results, depending upon their source.

MR. BUTLER: All of us agree that what we need most as a product of the school system is the ability to learn over and over again new skills, new techniques. Many of us have hunches about what subjects in the curriculum foster that ability. Perhaps through research we can pinpoint, for example, which junior high schools teaching which courses produce students who do better in high school, or which high schools teaching which courses at which point produce students who perform better during the rest of their high school years. Some think foreign languages produce the better students, some think it is algebra, some computer programming. But we need to know what those subjects are if research can tell us.

Another point I would like to make concerns the suggestion that what business wants from education or from collaboration with the schools is vocational training. When I was a high school senior in 1940, the Glenn L. Martin Aircraft Company of Maryland ran a Saturday morning course in blueprint reading at our high school. As it geared up to produce more airplanes for the war, it needed people who could come into the factory and read blueprints.

What we are talking about here is not vocational training. Industry can do that, not the schools.

We do not normally hire graduates right out of high school in our company. We hire only 1,200 people a year. We have approximately 40,000 people in the United States, and we pay wages well above average to get the kind of people we need. Yet we are intensely interested in public education.

51

Why? We are intensely interested in public education in Cincinnati because that is where we live and that is where we must get people to come to live. They want to live in a place with a good public school system—good in the very broadest sense of the word. We are interested in the national public education system because the products of that system elect the people who pass the laws determining the kind of society our company has to operate in. That is very important to us and brings into play our enlightened self-interest again.

I also think we should consider what women's lib has meant to public education. Understanding the effect of this movement on public education might shed some light on what changes we need to make to correct the problems that it may have created: for generations we drafted our public school teachers, in effect, and now we have gone to a concept of volunteer service. We ought to try to measure the effect of the change to see if we can find some corrective measures to help us deal with it.

BILL KOLBERG, National Alliance for Business: We have talked as if the two structures, business and public education, could somehow communicate very easily. Except for the larger companies in the United States, however, American business is not organized (this is an assumption on my part) well enough to be a partner day in and day out with the public school system. The school system, of course, is an institution in every community organized around a hierarchy and a structure.

I think we need a fair amount of research on structures like the Allegheny Conference and the New York Partnership. A number of major communities have developed an informed and an intelligent private sector partner with the public schools. In these communities businesses have traditionally provided wholesale merchandise, intelligent help, support, and first-class advice to the public school system. Why don't we have that everywhere? I don't know.

The institution of the private industry council is developing in a number of communities. A recent law, the Job Training Partnership Act, allows private sector volunteers to participate in groups responsible for running multibillion dollar programs. We in the business community pushed for that institutional change so that we could develop an effective private sector structure in those communities without such organizations as the Allegheny Conference. When business people are involved at the top level, with first-class staffs, such an institution can educate and inform those people about what goes on. We need that involvement on the private side, and we hope that from the Job Training Partnership Act will come a set of new institutions, either private industry councils or other kinds of organizations.

The businesses represented around the table today know how to get involved on their own; they have their resources. But we must realize that half the jobs in the United States are controlled by small businesses, those with 500 people or fewer. These do not have a training department or personnel depart-

52

ment. Although they do not know how to influence the public schools, they feel the same way that those of us employed by major institutions feel about the need for change in the public school system. They would work for change if they had an institution through which they could be heard and through which they could act.

I don't know if this adds up to a research agenda. I see a number of questions on institutional development on the private side, not on the public school side, that we all could benefit from. Those of us in the private sector could certainly benefit from further work on these issues.

MS. DANZBURGER: Some part of the educational agenda should be a longitudinal study of the results of partnerships, collaborations, and the involvement of different sectors, because the private sector measures results in a much shorter time frame.

Education cannot know its degree of success for a very long time. If a great deal of energy goes into creating these partnerships, then naturally we want to see some results. In working with a middle school, for instance, we would not be able to measure anything really meaningful except some short-term, quantifiable results. In terms of what we are talking about here, however, it will be ten years before we can know: did the young adults adapt in the workplace? Were they able to change jobs? Were they able to participate successfully in business training?

We don't conduct many such longitudinal studies in this country, but maybe major sectors are now poised to do business differently and to acknowledge that we cannot have instant feedback from the energy we expend.

DAVE BERGHOLZ, Allegheny Conference on Community Development: We have been working in a partnership program, an adopt-a-school kind of program, for a number of years. Of all the programs we have run, I think it has been the toughest one to make real.

On the subject of commitment and involvement, I would like to address the issue of substance: what makes a program meaningful, not only in the school but also in the business sector? We have found it very difficult to make the partnership effective. I believe that more blue smoke and mirrors are connected with the adopt-a-school programs than anything substantive. Somebody ought to look at those that work, why they do, and what the issues are that make those programs go. Many of us around the table may be deceiving ourselves about what that kind of program can accomplish.

We have the same sort of problem with a program we have been running for the past four years, a small grants-to-teachers program. I believe that if it makes the teacher happy and if it makes the kids in the class happy, it is a grant well spent. But those are not the questions I get. I get questions about what is coming out of the program—what innovation, what institutional change, what

53

curricular change, and so forth. It is not that I need to know how to make all of those things happen. I need to know whether the grants are of value in and of themselves, or whether they need to have other things attached. This is another programmatic research issue I am interested in.

The issue of the brokering or intermediary function that we have all talked about is important. Finding people able to do that isn't easy, and they may be born rather than made. If they could be made, though, what could we do to make them? What kind of training is involved? How can skillful mediators be identified? In which agencies and organizations might the people be placed to encourage effective relationships? Those issues are somewhat more pragmatic than other issues raised but do concern us.

DAVE RIPPEY, Aetna Institute for Corporate Education: In the course of sponsoring research within our company, I have noticed a peculiar phenomenon: academics or researchers who regard their techniques as rigorous or methodical confront managers who regard those same techniques as evidence of compulsive attention to work rather than to results. Or even worse, managers view the techniques as academic dilettantism or pastimes, not as avenues toward understanding the issues the researcher is addressing.

Those same academics believe that reporting their research is very important and that the research certainly merits enough pages to tell the story.

Managers who receive these reports believe that their business is to expedite information, and they like to handle information via extensive staff delegation or by the notorious one-page memo. Academics, then, tend to see business people as almost deliberately anti-intellectual or incurious. Those conflicting views made clear to me the importance of fostering conditions that allow collaborative research to happen.

The issue for all of us is usable knowledge. We need to know what can be produced and how quickly in terms of strong, comprehensive, and accessible models of planning and evaluation. Business people require something between pamphlet-variety descriptions and a twenty-pound document that will allow people at the operational level to proceed fairly quickly.

LARRY CUBAN, Stanford University: Not to talk seriously about elementary schooling only suggests a lack of seriousness about improvement of schooling. Why isn't business involvement moving down into the middle or elementary grades?

Although we all have our guesses about that, I think it is related to a whole set of assumptions. That is why I spent some time on assumptions. While I am motivated by urgency just like any practitioner or academic, I have found that urgency is no good. I spent twenty-five years in public education, and I have been urgent, just like other people have. But I have discovered that it is much better to define the issues and figure out where you're going to put your energies than just to go with the urgency.

As for adopting a school, I sense a general reluctance on the part of corporations to become involved at the elementary level, or to look at education over a long period of time. Now adopting elementary schools may occur and if it does, fine. But what I have read up to this point suggests the dominant thrust is toward high schools.

My second issue concerns the critical thinking skills, problem solving, and learning-to-learn. Three years ago NIE, which had a unit called Teaching and Learning, sponsored a conference in Pittsburgh on critical thinking skills. At that time the Arlington school board had mandated these skills as goals. Nonetheless, we discovered after five or six years of working on this issue that no one really knows what to do. You can't expect educators to know these things if the knowledge and application do not yet exist, or if no one knows what can be done with usable knowledge at the school level where educators face a whole complex of implementation problems.

And the last point deals with what was about an inch below the surface of the discussion but was not raised: what are the hidden conflicts that people do not really want to talk about? In talking about hidden conflicts, I refer to public policy, and that is why I am impressed with what the California Roundtable is doing even though I criticized it severely on a number of other points. It has either hired a lobbyist or asked CEOs to go to the legislature in California to lobby for a bill that will raise between $300 million and $700 million for stable, adequate funding of public schools in California. The issue of the use of public funds and the raising of public funds sets the business community and the educators at loggerheads. It raises the question of whether this current enthusiasm will produce something more substantial than adopting the schools, career days, or exchanges of personnel.

That kind of conflict is extremely important to articulate openly and to deal with openly, because what it really comes down to is it is going to cost a lot of money. A lot of the reports, for example, now talk about merit pay, which the head of the AFT has left open while other organizations have already come out against it. But any merit pay system or any elevation of public schools will depend upon higher teachers' salaries, either at the front end or at the back end of that salary schedule. There is no way to avoid that. Who is going to be in the coalition to support additional funds? And that conflict, I think, has to be raised openly.

One of the big things that we have to grapple with is how to sustain the state of collaboration that currently exists in the marketplace. When my staff and I contacted state education agencies across the country, we found that most of them were not doing anything toward business/education collaboration at that point or were like us, just initiating such activity. So, how do you maintain and sustain that momentum once it is going, and what incentives can be built into the design? While such incentives may not be as important for large

55

companies because they have great resources, for smaller business a lack of incentive is certainly a problem. Incentives, then, should be a topic, and also knowing what already has been done should be another.

DR. FOSTER: If you could get people like Brad Butler, Larry Cuban, and Bob Craig together on the issue of learning-to-learn, I think it would be productive for several reasons. First, new shifts are taking place. What concerns Mr. Butler is that he has middle managers who are adults who have got to learn-to-learn. What concerns Mr. Craig is that he is trying to find a way to be more systematic and to apply that kind of knowledge. What concerns Mr. Cuban is that researchers do not seem to come up with the kinds of propositions that we can test in a useful fashion.

If you can find ways of linking some of these issues, you can begin to build coalitions, and you may find the money. Someone has to take a look at the kind of research methodologies that are useful in these settings. That should happen when that kind of research is legitimized.

As for mediating structures, what if you transform the notion of school volunteers to include the whole range of issues that you now have? How do you take an organization that now exists and change it so that it begins to provide some of the kinds of people that Mr. Bergholz talked about? You can take a number of other traditional institutions or mediating structures and do the same thing.

MR. CALDWELL: I suggest researching a model based on past cases in similar areas to predict the likelihood of court intervention in the formation of partnerships. It is one thing for a state department of education—with the resources of the attorney general's office—to be hit with a major lawsuit. But it is quite another thing for a corporation to have to spend its resources, or its stockholders' resources defending possible lawsuits. This sort of thing is something that, quite frankly, is not very often done in the law. Although courts do not give advisory opinions, obviously, it might be interesting to think about a model.

SYLVIA WARE, American Chemical Society: We have talked a lot about communication between the business community and the educational community, but I would like to point out that the term "educational community" may mean different things in different areas of the country. The educational community is not synonymous with a teacher, and we do not know how teachers view school/business partnerships, which may have been in operation for ten or twenty years.

How have teachers responded to the historical record of such partnerships? Do teachers like them? Do they find them helpful? What characteristics of these particular programs would they like to see developed farther? Are teachers attracted to a community with these programs? Do they consider them evidence that they will be able to function effectively in such a community? Are they scared by such programs? Because the role of the teacher is central in the classroom, I think some attention should be paid to the teacher rather than to the educational community.

MR. HURWITZ: I would like to know what makes a teacher choose the profession? What discourages a person from entering the profession?

There is a great deal of talk about merit pay, differentiated pay, and the like. I am interested, however, in the system of perquisites for teachers. We talk about the need to reward teachers in particular areas, such as science and math. I am aware of several school systems in which the teachers enjoy such an elite status that rewarding them financially would be considered superfluous. They enjoy a particular kind of prestige that other teachers in the system simply do not enjoy.

At some time we may have to consider the question of merit pay, but I believe that a system of nonmonetary rewards and perquisites is an important research item.

RONI POSNER, American Vocational Association: For many years vocational educators have successfully collaborated with business and industry. From the beginning of the century, advisory councils and committees have set up programs, established standards, and requested the help of representatives from business and industry to develop curriculum. More recently, vocational education has played a role along with various state departments in bringing agencies together not only to attract new industry to states but also to maintain and expand existing industries.

The theme of our convention this year will be, in fact, industry/education collaboration. We are talking about collaboration. What does it mean when an industry "gets together" with a school, whether it is an elementary school, or a teacher, or a superintendent of schools, or even whether the collaboration occurs through the state legislature or through its policy on a component such as vocational education?

Research shows that one of the main reasons a company chooses to locate or expand in a particular location is the availability of a trained work force. I would therefore urge you to move, in addition to the focus on learning-to-learn, toward the basic skills and occupational skills that are demanded by industry not only for entry level but also for higher-level skilled workers.

ALAN GREEN, Education Facilities Lab: For the past few months I have been looking at collaborations in local communities. I do not know very much about megastructures and macro policy, but I know a little about what is going on at the local level. I do not want to leave this afternoon having thrown out the adopt-a-school concept.

I do not love that term by any means, but in many communities I observe that the relationships among a single school, its teachers, its kids, its parents, and one or more groups (corporations, perhaps) are a very important beginning point for the process of familiarization or for understanding each other. It is a very important first step in the evolutionary process. If we don't like adopt-a-school, per se, let's not get rid of it because I think it is a nice, benign, and terribly important place to start.

I do not think it is worth a lot of evaluation, though. The fact that a few people are coming together and talking with a few other people and that they are understanding more, building some confidence in the schools, that is enough in itself. At later stages perhaps we could examine the motivations.

Second, we should not assume that the leadership potential all lies within the corporate structure or in the corporate community. I observe that we have some very wonderful examples of health institutions, cultural institutions, civic organizations, and professional groups working with the schools. They are also providing leadership, they are also providing the neutral turf, and they are doing all these other things we are looking for. Let's cast our net fairly wide.

In a way, it comes back to a point made three hours ago when Mr. Caldwell referred to the fifty students whom he asked in class to say what they were going to do about the public schools. I wish one of those students had turned back to him and said, "And, Professor Caldwell, what has the Denver Bar Association done for the schools lately?"

DR. LEVINE: I would like to thank the authors for their cooperation and for their effort in preparing these papers and working with me in putting together this seminar with Nevzer Stacey. I also thank all of you participants for enriching the discussion and making this a very rewarding session.

PART THREE
Papers: Executive Summaries

*The following are summaries of the papers
presented and discussed at this conference.
The papers in their entirety are available from
the American Enterprise Institute.*

Barriers to Private Sector-Public School Collaboration: A Conceptual Framework

Marsha Levine

This paper suggests conceptual frameworks that may be helpful in addressing the question, Does public-private collaboration offer a viable approach to improving the quality of public education?

First, collaboration is defined and identified as one of several possible strategies the private sector might employ in its involvement with public schools. Certain characteristics of collaboration make it potentially a very effective form of involvement—for example, by reducing the isolation of schools and by establishing structural links for communication between sectors.

Second, three conceptual frameworks are then suggested that provide useful ways to think about private sector-public school collaboration: inter-institutional collaboration, public-private partnership, and a systems approach. Each of the frameworks offers a method for identifying a particular cross section of barriers and incentives. The perspective of interinstitutional collaboration focuses attention on the effects of environment and history, organizational factors, interorganizational processes, and the roles of individuals and linking structures. The framework of public-private partnerships introduces a more specific set of issues and factors related to balancing private sector interest and public sector responsibility and addresses them in the context of public schools. Several changes are identified as significant factors in developing public-private partnerships in education.

One change is the expansion of the definition of education beyond the traditional schooling in the usual time frames. This altered definition carries with it implications for shared institutional responsibilities and changes in public policy. Another change concerns the structural alterations in the economy that highlight the relationship between education and economic growth, emphasizing industry's interest in education. Last, demographic changes and a

61

low level of public support for public schools create a need for alliances with the private sector if the schools are to meet their human resource development goals.

The third framework focuses on schools as one system interacting with other sectors in society—that is, community and industry. Changes in one sector affect functions in the others. Because patterns have developed for relationships between schools and external organizations, perhaps business-education collaborations can profit from examining those relationships.

These conceptual frameworks offer useful guidelines for understanding and evaluating private sector involvement in public schools. Business-education partnerships, however, are pragmatic ventures. They are idiosyncratic and individual. Their goal is a mutually beneficial outcome. These frameworks can assist the process of collaboration but should not constrain it by any suggestion that partnerships must meet some set of uniform requirements.

This paper was prepared under National Institute of Education contract number NIE/P/0016.

Going Public:
A Labor-Education Perspective on
Private-Sector Involvement in the
Public Schools

Maurice Leiter

Four assumptions provide the context for this paper:

- NIE's interest in a research agenda for private sector involvement in public schools creates a necessary and timely *intellectual* (rather than political) atmosphere for discussion.
- The subject is not ephemeral or merely an outgrowth of President Reagan's priorities but rather a product of ongoing events and circumstances, such as the challenge of Japanese technology and productivity.
- There is a sufficient prehistory of collaboration of private sector and public schools to create a positive environment for analysis and to overcome "bandwagon" aspects.
- Schools, unions, and corporations are all nourished by economic health and opportunities for human and institutional growth as well as by feeling relevant and successful.

The central pragmatic question concerns what needs to be accomplished to make the public-private relationship of benefit to the whole society. Many examples of heightened commitment can be found on the part of labor and government to fostering links with the private sector in the related areas of education and economic development. Common interests bring public schools, labor unions, and corporations together with emphasis on mutual concerns rather than on historical differences. Increasingly, all parties have come to agree that our prosperity comes from a marriage of economic development and human capital formation. These grow out of a strong public education system sustaining a productive private sector, which in turn supports public education. One sector nurtures the other in a continuous cycle.

Incentives for collaboration and support of public schools by the private sector flow easily and sensibly from a recognition of mutual interest and shared goals and needs. These incentives are often national in scope and significance (in relation to economic development and productivity, for example). They are also frequently local as in the case of the business sector's need to attract workers, middle management, and customers—all of which are enhanced by sound public schools within a stable community environment. There are also significant long-range benefits to developing the capacity of population subgroups to take their place in society and in the world of work, because the labor force will be shrinking in the next decade at a time when a literate, skilled population will be more necessary than ever. The development of human potential through our public education system *has always been the basis of growth in our society.*

To assist private-public collaboration, we must also be willing to understand the barriers and biases that often make collaboration difficult. Many obstacles arise out of suspicions of motive or critical (often biased) perceptions of each other as, for example, in the widely held beliefs that business is narrowly profit-motivated or that public education is beyond redemption. Of course, examples of specific self-serving antisocial business activities and of particular public schools that are beset with difficulties are not hard to find. These half-truths or skewed perspectives can be overcome only by sticking to facts, working together, and recognizing that such examples are neither characteristic nor germane.

Other barriers to collaboration are products of organizational differences or simply of unfamiliarity. Making people in the private sector familiar with schools is a clear need. Overcoming assumptions that the private sector hierarchical model is effective within the school organism is another. Differences in outcome standards and over ways to assess productivity and an unwillingness to share risks or confront controversy jointly are also problems: businesses working with schools tend to avoid risk. In general, differences in customary operational models, organizational patterns, and assumptions about means and standards act as deterrents to collaboration.

Deeper thematic considerations that relate to the private sector role also need examination. Is there a contradiction between local "good works" and the public policy positions? Do businesses tend to "drive" the curriculum? Are schools overemphasizing the school-to-work modality?

Finally, a significant barrier is the very unwieldiness of *managing* private sector efforts. A system for coordination might better harness resources and increase beneficial effects.

Having a clear sense of an effective collaborative model is central to joint private sector-public school efforts. Sixteen criteria for effective collaboration are presented, for example, equity, joint development of activities, consensus, and respect for each other's universe, needs, and political pressures. Two examples within the author's experience of private sector efforts to work with public schools are described in detail and are measured against the criteria for collaboration to illustrate the differences of approach and to argue for the collaborative model as the way to strengthen partnerships.

Many questions for further study and analysis remain—policy questions, questions of impact, and data-gathering matters. The key policy question is still, What are effective roles for the private sector with respect to the public schools? On the impact level, the paper asks, Has private sector support of specific activities generated pupil or other outcomes *not otherwise possible*? Resource allocation studies would also be helpful. For example, Have urban schools experienced increased benefit, or have other social responsibility beneficiaries experienced a comparable decline in support? Further study and policy analysis are critically needed, because so much has happened so fast.

"Going public" has already shown itself to be largely beneficial. The logic of common interest joins private and public constituencies. Strengthening the nurturing cycle of public education and private economic growth helps everyone. The collaborative model is recommended whatever the level or locus of activity to ensure the strongest and longest-lasting effects. All activity should be encouraged whether site-specific or otherwise, but, in the final analysis, it is probable that the private sector can be most effective in broad-based efforts to support public education, strengthen overall standards, and provide adequate resources. This effort requires coordination nationally by individual business leaders and by consortia of high-level corporate officials. Working together, the private sector and the public schools can open areas of partnership far beyond the present dimensions.

This paper was prepared under National Institute of Education contract number NIE/P/0012.

Corporate Involvement in Public Schools: A Practitioner-Academic's Perspective

Larry Cuban

In discussing the current enthusiasm for business-education collaboration, the author uses his experience of seven years as a school superintendent to stress the self-evident point that a school district is inevitably part of a business community as a corporation buying and selling and employing members of the community. Yet a school district differs substantially from the corporate sector because of its public obligations and the use of tax funds to discharge those obligations.

In making that point he also reviews the last century of business-education cooperation, which produced the vocationalizing of high schools, a mission approved and accepted by the general public. That review of the history produced a number of echoes familiar to the observers of the current corporate interest in schooling.

He then compares previous efforts and the present one in terms of their magnitude, motives, and assumptions to determine where the past attempts converge with or diverge from the current enthusiasm. He asks whether there are new directions being explored. In magnitude and motives, there are definite similarities to previous collaborative efforts. Major differences reside in the level of corporate involvement (higher and more extensive in the earlier decades of the century) and the focus (shift from concentration on vocational preparation to current interest in general education).

In critically examining the set of assumptions embedded in contemporary joint efforts at improving the high school, he analyzes such widely held beliefs as that lack of high school training causes unemployment; improving high school students' test performance will produce better-trained graduates; high-technology requirements demand major curricular changes; and business support will help restore confidence in public schools. The last assumption concerning restoration of confidence in public schools, he believes, is the most substantial contribution that joint corporate-education coalitions can make to the nation. In reaching that conclusion, he also acknowledges the divergent interests and hidden conflicts embedded in that coalition, for example, business's concern about efficient uses of tax funds and public schools' need for stable funding.

In helping to restore confidence in public schools, corporate involvement also holds the potential for altering current arrangements in public schools insofar as teacher tenure, evaluation of school district graduates and their contributions to the community, and a reassessment of how schools can improve their performance in teaching students to think critically. The trade-offs anchored in collaborative ventures between business and schools are discussed within the context of his service as a school superintendent.

This paper was prepared under National Institute of Education contract number NIE/P/0014.

An Equitable Framework for Corporate Participation in the Public Schools

Richard Allen Caldwell

Critical to America's need for a technologically literate and economically productive work force is the redefinition of the relationship between private industry and the public schools. Simply stated, the educational system cannot remain isolated from the needs, priorities, and intentions of the corporate sector.

Increasingly, it is recognized that there is a distinct lack of clear national policy with respect to the educational foundation required for those who will work in the high-technology or service-related industries of the future. Equally important is the question of the degree of *legally permissible* cooperation between corporations and the schools. The failure to explore the idea of partnerships between public schools and private industry more fully, or to create supportive legal mechanisms, may accentuate a growing "technological illiteracy," consign many of our deserving citizens to unemployment or under-employment, and result in the presence in society of substantial numbers of people only marginally qualified to function in a competitive economic environment.

Governance in America is based on the notion that we are a "nation of laws and not of men." Nevertheless, our legal system contains a great deal of flexibility, which is the result of a unique constitutional structure. Subject to state and federal constitutional restrictions, interpretations, and changing definitions of substantive justice, the state legislative body possesses complete power over the schools. If it chose to do so, for example, the state legislature could change local school boundaries, prescribe curriculum, set school accreditation standards, enhance school safety requirements, alter teacher certification requirements, and set teacher tenure requirements. This control by the state legislature is subject, however, to review by the state and federal courts for violation of constitutional rights.

State laws concerning schools generally provide broad guidelines; thus, control of public education means little in the abstract. The structural details come from either state education departments or from local district implementation. The local school districts, through powers delegated from the state legislature, carry the major responsibility for day-to-day operations.

Corporate aid to the public schools, in whatever form, must fit into a preexisting legal framework. Legal questions surrounding private-public partnerships in education have as their basis a recognition of the gradual recasting of fundamental distinctions between the private and public sectors.

The central argument of this paper is that the most significant legal barrier to the deepening involvement of corporations with the public schools is, ultimately, the problem of finding constitutional mechanisms for the *fair* and *equitable* distribution of corporate resources in aid of education. It will be argued that corporate contributions are to be welcomed, from a policy perspective, if they can be made within an equal protection framework that does not enhance the position of some students, or some school districts, at the expense of others.

The ideas of equity, fairness, and equality are central values in the American ideological system. Yet, there is considerable and sharp disagreement about what these values mean in an educational context. This conflict is derived from the fact that the *objectives* of education have long been a source of intense policy dispute. This is so because education can serve as an equalizing or a leveling social force, or it can function as an unfair selection mechanism that perpetuates existing patterns of inequality and lack of opportunity.

American courts have been closely involved in deciding major issues of education policy and in overriding the total autonomy of local and state authorities. In the main, courts have concerned themselves with two problems: (1) eliminating segregation in the schools; and (2) equalizing educational opportunities. Thus, the rejection of the "separate but equal doctrine," in *Brown* v. *Board of Education of Topeka,* was followed by intense litigation about disparities in school finance schemes. Because most elementary and secondary school revenues are generated by local property taxes and the amount and value of taxable property vary tremendously from one school district to another, the unequal distribution of resources works to the considerable disadvantage, it is alleged, of residents of poorer school districts.

The many school finance cases are important because corporate contributions to schools, no matter how they are structured, may very well be likened to a kind of *finance,* that is, funding of a new type that could be subject to judicial review by interested courts. The central issue in the present discussion is the need to find a way to *balance* the possible *right* to an equally financed education against what could be defined as an evolving state *interest* in promoting an education policy that may result in better training, economic growth, and higher employment prospects for graduates. Simply stated, there is clearly a state interest in encouraging *quality* education, even at the expense of abstract notions of perfect *equality*. Indeed, additional educational opportunities, made possible by enlightened, even self-interested, corporate initiatives that are nondiscriminatory in intent, may result in *greater* overall equity. Better schools are in the public interest.

If better education is the result of new kinds of partnerships between businesses and schools, then a strict, judicially based, test of "contributional equality" may not be required by even very broad interpretations of the Fourteenth Amendment's equal protection clause. It is the position of this paper, however, that reclaiming excellence in education, through breaking down some barriers between public and private, will require a heightened commitment to *equity* on the part of corporations, in order to avoid, at some point in the future, a substantial measure of judicial scrutiny and intervention.

This paper was prepared under National Institute of Education contract number NIE/P/0015.

Incentives and Barriers to Private Sector Involvement in Public Schools: A Corporation's Perspective

Marcia Appel and Susan Schilling

The area of greatest opportunity for private sector-public school cooperation is in improving the educational process itself through the introduction of technology. Computer-based education systems developed by industry have for years demonstrated the ability to teach, train, motivate, and build the skills of groups as diverse as engineering students in college, disadvantaged young people, airline flight crews, and automotive workers. What is needed now is a process to speed the acceptance and use of computer-based learning in public schools generally.

The report of the National Commission on Excellence in Education makes clear that a restructuring of the U.S. school system is in order, with the paramount goal being an across-the-board increase in the quality, availability, and effectiveness of instruction. Standing in the way is a tradition that emphasizes "group" education at the expense of the individual. Under this method, thirty students in a class are exposed to precisely the same material for the same time, tested on it, evaluated relative to one another's score, and then promoted or held back accordingly.

The result is a process that limits exceptional learners, inhibits slower students, and favors an orderly processing of the group over the educational development of each student. Moreover, in designing lessons and handling administrative matters, the teacher is asked to be a jack-of-all-trades and, not surprisingly, can be a master of none.

Computer-based instruction, however, offers the potential for tailoring an individual learning program to each student and for delivering it in a way that is motivational, interactive, self-paced, and competency based, meaning that material must be mastered before a lesson continues. In addition, the computer relieves teachers of many administrative chores, from record keeping to test scoring, freeing them to spend more time teaching and providing individual attention to students.

71

Control Data Corporation, as one example, developed the PLATO computer-based system and in the past ten years has made it the centerpiece of for-profit training applications ranging from computer programming and robotics instruction to basic literacy skills for unemployed teen-agers. A total of more than 1,200 courseware titles are available, representing almost 15,000 hours of instruction.

The private sector, which competes on the basis of its workers' skills and which spends $100 billion annually for employee training, has embraced computer-based systems such as PLATO—as have some schools and colleges. But some segments of traditional secondary and postsecondary education have resisted the technology, with opposition coming from teachers who fear for their jobs and school districts that fear "dehumanizing" effects of computers. In practice, computers have functioned as teaching tools, not replacements, and the primary response of students already at ease with computer video technology is enhanced motivation and excitement.

By working with selected schools and developing an education process that mixes technology and people in the most effective combination, Control Data feels it has a formula for computer-based education applicable on a broad scale. It is at the point of making this learning technology an integral part of the U.S. education system that the interests of public and private sectors coincide. Sophisticated development and implementation of such a basic change will require extensive collaboration, but the rewards inherent in a more productive, quality-oriented education system make the effort worthwhile and necessary.

This paper was prepared under National Institute of Education contract number NIE/P/0017.

Values and Incentives to Business-Education Collaboration: A Corporate Perspective

Badi G. Foster and David R. Rippey

In the past few years, a great deal of attention has been given to issues of collaboration between businesses and education. Despite this attention, questions remain as to whether collaboration is just another word for some fundamental practices of responsible citizenship and good management, or whether it represents some new form of the social contract. The purpose of this paper is to discuss some of the dynamics of business-education collaboration from the authors' point of view as educators recently transplanted into a very large corporation.

The authors begin by pointing out that there is no shared philosophy or methodology of education among all private sector institutions. Business reportedly spends roughly $30 billion per year for education and training. Employer-sponsored education usually stems from such business requirements as the need to orient new employees to the organization, to absorb rapid technological change, to reduce outside costs for education, and so forth. The Aetna Institute for Corporate Education will address these needs as well as those arising out of the transformation of the company from a provider of insurance to a provider of financial services. The mission of the institute is to meet the business-related educational needs of Aetna Life and Casualty.

A number of environmental factors affect planning around education and training in most corporations. These factors include changes in the labor force relative to age, skills, mobility, education, and racial and ethnic composition. Corporations can generally take one of four options in response to these changes:

- strengthen the ways in which they currently supplement education
- engage in school-business partnerships
- provide the equivalent of public or other education themselves

73

- do nothing at all about the problems of education and training outside of the corporate setting

The Aetna Institute for Corporate Education includes an External Program Unit. The mission of the unit is to develop external education programs and services serving both Aetna's human resources needs and corporate public involvement strategies. Current unit activities encompass the Hartford School Business Collaborative, area colleges and universities, and community-based organizations. The unit has developed some perspectives on what collaboration is and how it works. These include:

- The objective in any collaborative effort is to accommodate rather than exclude competing definitions of "the problem."
- It is important neither to overestimate nor to underestimate the capacity of any single organization, philosophy, or program to provide solutions to community problems.
- Measures of progress and success of collaboration need to be established.
- Collaboration is facilitated by the establishment of neutral turf.
- Collaboration requires regular, if not full-time attention.
- Internal collaboration in complex organizations is as important to manage as collaboration among institutions.

Successful development of policy and practice concerning collaboration hinges on the effective use of research. Effectiveness begins with a sense of history that allows planners to make the best use of existing research. Generating new knowledge will involve some reexamination of the enterprise of research itself. Problems arise because much of the language in many of the techniques of social science research have little currency in the private sector. Conversely, researchers often think that business people resist—to their own detriment—the potential benefits of research. Given these opposing views, the issue of facilitating conditions that allow collaborative research to take place becomes extremely important. Academics and private sector representatives can be partners in rethinking the design and implementation of research models.

Index

Selected AEI Publications

AEI Associates Program